Anonymous

Centennial services of the Fourth Presbyterian Church of the city of New York

Anonymous

Centennial services of the Fourth Presbyterian Church of the city of New York

ISBN/EAN: 9783337261160

Printed in Europe, USA, Canada, Australia, Japan

Cover: Foto ©Lupo / pixelio.de

More available books at **www.hansebooks.com**

CENTENNIAL SERVICES

OF THE

FOURTH PRESBYTERIAN CHURCH

OF THE CITY OF NEW-YORK

OCTOBER 25 — NOVEMBER 1
1885

1785

The Fourth Presbyterian Church,

Thirty-fourth Street,
West of Broadway,
New York City.

Joseph R. Kerr, D.D., Pastor.

1885

Preliminary Proceedings.

PURSUANT to a notice from the pulpit, a meeting of the congregation was held in the Lecture-room on Wednesday evening, June 16, 1885, for the purpose of considering the propriety of celebrating the centennial of the church.

After organization and some explanatory words by the pastor, it was resolved to approve the suggestions of the Session for holding special public services, beginning on the twenty-fifth of October, continuing through the week, and closing on the first of November; and a General Committee, representing the older members and families of the church, was appointed to make all necessary arrangements.

General Committee.

HONORARY.

Rev. John Spaulding, D.D.,   Joseph G. Harrison,
Rev. Joseph R. Kerr, D.D.,   William Eagle,
David Morrison.

RULING ELDERS' WIDOWS.

Mrs. John Aitken,   Mrs. Samuel Kydd,
Mrs. James Allen,   Mrs. William Dalrymple,
Mrs. John Kirkpatrick,   Mrs. John Iverach,
Mrs. James Stuart.

ELDERS.

Archibald McLintock,
James Kydd.

TRUSTEES.

John L. Cameron,
John H. Allen.

CONGREGATION.

Robt. Marshall,   Mrs. Robert Dinwiddie,
James McGay,   Mrs. William Harrison,
John McIntire,   Mrs. Frederick Blume,
Andrew Craig,   Mrs. C. W. Cameron,
James Nicholson,   Mrs. A. M. Stewart,
Walter Stevenson,   Mrs. Thomas Kirkpatrick,
Thomas D. Brown,   Mrs. James Cameron,
William A. Morrison,   Mrs. James Kydd,
William Allan,   Mrs. R. A. Dorman,
Thomas T. Allan,   Mrs. Elizabeth Hooker,
William Taylor,   Mrs. J. B. Mattison,
Henry Paige,   Miss Margaret F. Haggart,
Duncan Macfarlane,   Miss Maggie S. Strachan,
James A. Craig,   Miss Ella I. Morrison,
Thomas Cochrane,   Miss Grace L. Ritchie.

ARCHIBALD McLINTOCK, Chairman.

Andrew Craig, Secretary.   John H. Allen, Treasurer.

Finance Committee.

John H. Allen, Chairman,
Robert Marshall,
John McIntire,
Thomas D. Brown,
John L. Cameron,
William Allan,
Mrs. William Harrison,
Mrs. Frederick Blume,
Mrs. Thomas Kirkpatrick,
Mrs. R. A. Dorman,
James A. Craig.

Printing Committee.

James Kydd, Chairman,
John L. Cameron,
James Nicholson,
Duncan Macfarlane,
William A. Morrison.

Sociable Committee.

James McGay, Chairman,
James A. Craig,
William Taylor,
Thomas Cochrane,
Thomas T. Allan,
Mrs. A. M. Stewart,
Mrs. William Harrison,
Mrs. James Kydd,
Mrs. Elizabeth Hooker,
Miss Maggie S. Strachan,
Miss Grace L. Ritchie,
Miss Ella I. Morrison,
Mrs. James Cameron.

Welcome Committee.

Archibald McLintock, Ch'n,
Robert Marshall,
Thomas D. Brown,
James Kydd,
John McIntire,
Henry Paige,
Mrs. Robert Dinwiddie,
Mrs. C. W. Cameron,
Mrs. William Harrison,
Mrs. Frederick Blume,
Mrs. J. B. Mattison,
Miss Margaret F. Haggart.

Decoration Committee.

Andrew Craig, Chairman,
John H. Allen,
Walter Stevenson,
Mrs. R. A. Dorman,
Mrs. James Kydd,
Miss Maggie S. Strachan,
Mrs. Thomas Kirkpatrick.

Officers of the Church.
1885.

Rev. Joseph R. Kerr, D.D., Pastor.

RULING ELDERS.

Archibald McLintock.
Joseph A. MacDonald.
James R. Cuming.
Henry Cole Smith.

James Kydd.
Alexander Mackenzie.
John H. MacDonald.
Frederick Blume,
   Clerk of Session.

BOARD OF TRUSTEES.

David Morrison, Pres.
Francis Pringle, Vice-Pres.
John L. Cameron, Sec'y.
John H. Allen, Treas.
Joseph G. Harrison.
Marcus B. Bookstaver.

Minister at the West Side Chapel.

Rev. W. J. MacDowell.

The Invitation.

You are cordially invited to participate in the special Centennial Services of this Church, beginning on Sabbath, October the Twenty-fifth, continuing through the week and concluding on Sabbath, November the First, Eighteen Hundred and Eighty-five.

TILDEN FOUNDATION

The Church at the Corner of Grand and Mercer Streets.

Sabbath, October 25, 1885.

DIVINE SERVICE AT 11 A. M.

SERMON BY THE REV. JOHN THOMSON, D. D.

DIVINE SERVICE AT 4 P. M.

HISTORICAL SERMON BY THE PASTOR.

The Revs. S. D. Alexander, D.D., E. D. G. Prime, D. D., John Spaulding, D. D., and the Rev. W. J. Macdowell took part in these services.

SERMON

BY THE

REV. JOHN THOMSON, D. D.

The Glory which Thou gavest me I have given them.—JOHN xvii. 22.

AT the close of His farewell address to His disciples, and in full view of His betrayal and approaching sufferings, the Lord offered the prayer which this chapter contains. It is commonly called His intercessory prayer, as it refers mainly to "those whom the Father had given Him" that their number might be completed, and so the glorious body that, in the eternal purpose of God, they compose, be finished, and made perfect. You observe that He intercedes on their behalf that they may be sanctified, brought together, made one, and finally that they may be made perfect in glory. In the purpose of God, which was fully and absolutely known to Him, His glory as the appointed Mediator was secured. It was His glory. He saw it before Him, and longed for its full possession. The glory of all whom the Father had given Him was involved in the same divine purpose. His own glory as the Father's gift, and their glory in Him as the elect of God, and the objects of His redeeming love. Through the intervening veil of His unparalleled sufferings the Lord saw this glory as all His own, and as entrusted to Him for them, and set it before Him as a possession so sure, so absolutely certain, that He may be here understood as speaking of it by way of anticipation. It hangs on no conceivable contingency, nothing can divert it from Him, nor hinder His people's participation in it, and therefore He is fully warranted in speaking of it as He here does,—as a possession received by Him, and by Him bestowed on them. By the Father's purpose it was already His. In His intention it was already theirs. "The glory which thou gavest me I have given them."

Let the question then be: What is this glory of which the Lord here speaks as having been received of the Father, and bestowed by Him upon those whom the Father had given Him? It can in no sense be what may be called His essential glory, or the glory that belongs to

His uncreated and eternal godhead. For of it He says that it was given Him of His Father,— the glory which thou gavest me. His omnipotence, omniscience, and omnipresence *(e. g.)* are His glory; and this He was pleased occasionally to display; as in turning the water into wine, and in raising Lazarus from the dead, in both which He is said to have manifested His glory. But this glory is not a derived glory; nor one of which He could say, "the glory which thou gavest me"; for it is inherent in His very nature. He may veil it, or He may hold it for a season in abeyance, but He cannot even for a moment divest himself of it, without at the same time divesting himself of His being. The glory here spoken of, then, is a glory which belongs to Him in His mediatorial character and office; for only in this character is the Son subordinate to the Father. Some are of opinion that the glory here referred to was the power of working miracles by which His cause and kingdom were declared to men; but although it did please Him to invest His first disciples with this power, I am fully persuaded that this is not the glory here indicated, for He prays in this chapter for His disciples through all the ages, and we know that during many ages of the past that power has been withheld from the church, and I see not that we have any warrant whatever to expect that it shall ever again be bestowed.

It was not, then, His essential or inherent glory, for that was never given, and it was not the power of miracles, for that has long been withdrawn; but it may be referred with greater show of reason to the privileges which Christ subjectively hath, and which He is graciously pleased to bestow upon them that love Him. *E. g.* We are sons of God, as well and as truly, though not in the same intimacy of relation as He, yet are we joint heirs with Him in glory; with Him we shall be glorified; with Him we shall be raised up; with Him we shall reign; with Him we shall sit on thrones of glory, judging the world. ALL WITH HIM! beloved, with Him! Oh, why is it that we go so bowed down with our temptations and unworthiness—our heads like a bulrush—amid the light and hope of a divine declaration like this? Is it the infirmity only of His blood-bought children that they rise not up to the true dignity of God's high calling, and that they prefer, on some vague ground or other, to go mourning all their days, rather than in possession and exercise of the joy of faith in their ever-living Head, to exhibit the same in their walk and conversation before the world to the praise of the glory of His grace? Oh, let as many as have this hope in Him, and have been taught by His spirit to know and receive these sayings of His,—let us arise, brethren, and shake ourselves from the dust, and put on the beautiful garments that He offers from His own wardrobe, and stand forth before the world as the sons of God and joint heirs with the Lord Jesus Christ. To do less than this is to dishonor our Lord, to pour contempt on His word, and to weaken our own testimony to His grace, and to veil unwarrantably the glory which He hath given us.

What, then, is this glory which He hath received of the Father and hath given to us? Most certainly the very choice and appointment of the eternal Son to accomplish the redemption of men was itself a glory that was given Him by the Father. He saw and felt and was fully conscious of the glory that enwrapped Him when He thus stated broadly and distinctly the nature of His own mission in the world. "The Son of Man is come to seek and to save that which was lost." And again: "God so loved the world that He gave His only begotten Son, that whosoever believeth in Him should not perish, but have everlasting life." In the position which He occupied in coming into the world as a saviour and a redeemer of lost sinners of mankind, He was there by the Father's choice and appointment. He took not upon himself the honor of the priestly office. He was chosen to it,— called to it,— appointed to it,— and so is He God's gift. This glory, then, is conferred upon Him; He received it of the Father. In one very high and distinguishing sense Christ was glorified, even when the Lord made to meet upon Him all the iniquities of the elect; and when He bare our sins in His own body on the tree,— for this was done that the lost might be saved, that the wanderers might be restored to their Father's house. Never was higher office known in the universe of God, and never can there be, than that which, on the Father's election, the Son undertook to fulfill. About its darkest humiliations, its deepest sufferings, even to that of the death on the cross, there is a glory which no creature could have borne. Even before His sufferings began, and during all the years through which they were extended, the glory of mediation was His by the Father's gift, and given to Him in order to the salvation of fallen men. It was His glory to glorify the Father in the redemption of the purchased possession. The end of His appointment by the Father is distinctly stated, and it is a glorious one for man, and a glorious one for God. Just grasp it, beloved! To save the lost, to ransom the slave, to deliver the lawful captive, to storm the very stronghold of the Prince of Darkness, to hurl him from his long-usurped supremacy, and to set the prisoners free. What to it are all the noble schemes of benevolence and mercy in which the generations of men have been engaged? Bring them all together, with all the resources they have commanded, and all the energy they have called into action, and all the benefits they have sought to secure for human kind; rid them even of all impurities that may have mingled with them from age to age, of human pride and ambition and selfishness; put every one of them in its very best and broadest and brightest light, and what are they when set in contrast with the mission of the Son of God?

We honor the brave and the good of the past, whose labors and sufferings and self-sacrifice have stirred our hearts and shamed our selfishness; we sing their praises and talk of their mighty deeds; we cover their infirmities with the mantle of charity, and record their virtues on the rock forever; or, if alive and laboring still in the cause of humanity, we follow them in the paths they are pursuing; never more disposed to applaud than just when we see them suffering and enduring hardship in the warfare to which they have given themselves. We know all this, and can enter intelligently into it. Nor would I pluck one star from the crown that sits upon the brow of the great and the good, nor diminish in aught the glory they have so hardly won; and all the more, when I see of many of them that they have renounced comfort and ease, their right to enjoy which was unquestionable, and have not shrunk from hard ways, and toilsome and comfortless, nor from neglect and reproach in order to work out some good for their generation. Do but apply this by way of feebly illustrating the mission of Christ into the world, and His complete and accepted discharge of the same, and say, was there ever a grander or more gracious mission to upraise the fallen, to save the lost? And where, in any case, have been the sorrows like unto His sorrow, or humiliation or sufferings in any sense parallel to those which He stooped to endure? The end which He came to work out is one which admits of no parallel between it and any other even the very highest and purest of philanthropic achievements which it has been given to man to work out; and the same is true of His sufferings, in drinking the last bitter dregs of which He proclaimed himself the conqueror. The end proposed throws back a marvelous flood of glory upon all His humiliations and sufferings, so that the very crown of thorns stands possessed of a glory unknown to any other of His many crowns. And this glory He had received from the Father, and it shone around Him, even in the darkest hours of His humiliation.

From this point of view may we not inquire whether there is not a glory which Christ has bestowed and continues to bestow upon all His true disciples? I think, from what has been said, the answer is clear. Was Paul correct when he wrote thus of himself and his brethren in the faith of Christ, " None of us liveth to himself"? What was his meaning in such words as these, but that there is a wide sweeping gulf between the end which the children of this world propose to themselves and the high aim which the follower of Christ lives to achieve? Time bounds the desires and efforts of the one,—those of the other are concerned with time only as the probation for, the vestibule of, a coming eternity. The one knows what self-denial for the Lord's sake is, and self-sacrifice and self-mortification. Such phrases as these (the crucifying of the flesh, the death of our natures to sin) are not at all strange or unmeaning terms to them, while the other knows nothing about them. Now whence comes this? Not certainly from nature, and not from birth or blood, and not from circumstances, as our own experience not less than the lively oracles of God clearly shows. No, but from the Lord. Not a Christian but gives all the glory of his second birth, and better nature, and consecrated life, to the Lord. He it is who gives to every follower of His the inclination and the power to be of use to his brethren; who puts it into his heart to deny himself and to sacrifice himself for his brethren's good; who fills a man's soul with that spirit which leads him to spend and be spent for the advancement of the kingdom of God. Christ gives this spirit to His own redeemed ones, and in giving it He makes them partakers of His own glory.

He gave it to the holy apostle of the Gentiles — Paul — when truly He breathed into his nostrils the breath of life, and he became a living soul. Not till then had Paul begun to live. The very highest form of life with which he had up to that time been allied was the life of a religious party or sect — or perhaps we should call it a national life — of a politico-religious character. Beyond this his ambition had never risen, and even then self was confessedly very largely the heart and soul of it. But from the moment of his second birth another spirit possessed him, the narrow bounds of time as the theater of human action and endurance faded away in the brightness of a near and ever visible eternity. And then also when the commandment came Paul died; but out of that death sprang life — life that rejoiced to expend itself in great labors which have glorified his name — life that rose above the ease and the comfort of the individual, that broke away from the fetters of party and fashion, and spurned the still stronger bands of national exaltation and glory — that rose into regions of thought and of action akin to those of Him who, though in the form of God, rejoiced in the title of the "Son of Man." It is not left to us to conjecture whence so great a change originated, or how it came to be wrought in Paul. He himself attributed its origin and preservation and power to Christ—Christ given *for him*, Christ living in him. The same spirit that animated Christ working also according to the measure of the gift of Christ in Paul. To lift up Christ Jesus the Lord as the friend of sinners, to proclaim the great salvation procured by His death, to invite the weary and heavy-laden to look unto Him and be saved,—such was Paul's philanthropic life. Ye know to what perils it exposed him. It is enough to mark now that this high and distinguishing glory was Christ's gift to Paul, and not to him only, but to those other brethren, the early evangelists, who, in the face of opposition and at the sacrifice of every outward comfort, proclaimed among the nations the Gospel of Peace. He gave it also to that grand host of confessors and martyrs who gladly suffered the loss of all things, and counted not their lives dear unto them, that they might testify to God among their fellow-men. He has given it to a long list of faithful servants, whose names adorn the history of the church, and to whom the defense and the progress of the truth from age to age has been owing. He has given it to many whose names are unrecorded, but who in their quiet spheres have labored and endured for the profit of those around them, and for the honor of their Master and of His cause. He has given it to many a pastor on whom the breath of popular applause has never rested — who has gone in and out among the people of his charge, telling to them and to their children the good news of God's kingdom, till, his work at length ended, he has gone down to his rest, and now sleeps in peace amid the people over whose eternal well-being his whole heart yearned. He has given it to many a one ministering by the bed-side of the poor and needy, and to many a ministering physician at the couch of the dying; aye, and He has given it to many of those poor and suffering ones who have benefited mankind by the patience and meekness and holy consistency of their lives, and by the depth of their sympathy and prayers. So have I seen in the abodes of humble life, and in the chamber of intense and long-protracted suffering, a sunshine and sweet peace to which the dwellings of the ungodly have been strangers — a sunshine which has made its power felt in circles far remote.

This is of the Lord. Christ has given, as it were, a portion of His own glory to those in every walk of life to whom He has granted His own spirit of beneficence, and who are striving, according to their opportunities, to perpetuate and diffuse its blessings. The world may not see it;

but the Lord sees it, and His angels also are witnesses of it. Those even to whom it is given may not always see it in themselves. Indeed, they who are most largely endowed with the gift are, in general, the least conscious of its possession. But the bliss and the felicity of the spirit of Christ they are enabled to feel within them, for "in keeping His commandments is great reward." Bear in mind that grand and glorious utterance concerning Christ: "He went about continually doing good." What a life was that! Worthy of all praise, and surely of all imitation. And such is just the life of all that are in Christ. They "walk not after the flesh, but after the spirit." Yes, the very spirit of Christ, for "he that hath not the spirit of Christ is none of His." And "if any man be in Christ, he is a new creature"; "old things are passed away, behold all things are become new." The foot-prints of the ever-blessed Lord form the path of all in whom the spirit dwells. They follow Him, neither to atone for sin nor to mediate with God for man. He has finished all that, but they follow Him in His blessed pathway of beneficence, denying themselves, and even gladly submitting to scorn and reproach and death itself when called thereto by God. In none of His incommunicable attributes and excellencies can they ever reach unto Him. They can never be omnipotent, omniscient, nor omnipresent, nor have they a desire to be so; but in blessing others, as it was His delight to do; in doing good, even the highest good, to others, as it was His work and life to do; in exposing themselves to hardship and suffering, to do so the more effectively, and to do this, in His spirit and for His glory,—this is the life-work, not only of His ministers, but of all that are called to be saints. And truly about such a life, how lowly soever may be its sphere, there is a glory that pales the luster of crowns and coronets. To be blessed of the Lord with saving grace is, indeed, a priceless privilege; and only second to that is the blessing of being made a blessing. They that are rich through God's bounty are doubly blessed by having it in their hearts to make others happy out of their abundance, and they that have signal talents are doubly rewarded by having it in their hearts to devote them to the service of God among men. Though, to fulfill this glory, it does not require, in every case, either great riches or great talents; yet this it does require always — a new heart and a right spirit. This it is, and no gift of earthly kind, that gives to every action and utterance of the Christian the true celestial ring. And this is Christ's benison, and in this consists the believer's likeness to the Lord. And thus it is that I understand the words of the text, "The glory which thou gavest me I have given them." Think of it, then, beloved! No disciple is exempted from this God-like and glorious work. God's election of them in Christ is to the end that they may bring forth enduring fruit, and much of it, for "herein is my Father glorified, that ye bear much fruit."

God's gifts to men are manifold. None are without some one gift or other, in greater or less degree, which, when discovered and exercised, is designed to benefit others. The grace of God does not destroy these gifts, but rather develops them and gives them direction and strength; and in no higher or more glorious work can any of them be employed than in that of ameliorating the condition of men. So in our more sober and unselfish moods we think and feel, and rightly, too; for so to do is Christ-like. "He spared not himself, but gave himself up for us all." How, then, can we better use His gifts to us than in maintaining and extending His blessed cause? Oh, that it were written over every dwelling, over every workshop, over every church—"None of us liveth to himself." None that enter here live for themselves; we live for each other; we live for our Lord; we live to perpetuate the name and memory and example of Him who went about, continually doing good. We are true socialists, without being communists; we believe in the communion of saints, because we rejoice in communion with God. Partakers by His grace of that glory which He received of the Father, we cannot, we would not, but walk in His footsteps, counting it our highest honor and joy to do good in His name, and to communicate of His gifts entrusted to us. Lord Jesus, help us, by Thy spirit, thus to live, that we may benefit the world by our presence in it, that we may bless it by our example, and hasten on the day of its gladsome restoration, when its kingdoms shall have become the kingdoms of our Lord and of His Christ, to whom be glory, for ever and ever.

Our fathers began this blessed work in this city a hundred years ago, when New-York was but "a little one," and their own resources were limited — when they assembled together on the Lord's Day in private houses, and in prayer and supplication and thanksgiving laid the foundations of the goodly edifice in which we are to-day assembled. From Nassau street to Grand street, and thence across Broadway, still in Grand street, and thence to this noble thoroughfare and to our present location,—the enlarging demands of business and an increasing population rendering these changes desirable and necessary. Born out of the throes of Revolutionary times, OUR LITTLE ONE has passed through repeated strifes of war and fire and pestilence, —going on from strength to strength as its years were multiplied, giving forth with ever-increasing energy a sweet savor of Jesus Christ,— holding aloft its banner of truth, and receiving from the ever-open hand of God the supplies that have preserved it from pandering to popular sensationalism on the one hand, and, on the other, safe from the demands of money-lenders — the rocks on which so many well-intentioned efforts have suffered shipwreck.

From the beginning of my ministry to this congregation I was made to see that I was surrounded by men and ministered to by women who feared the Lord and spake often one toward another of the great things and rich provisions of His kingdom, and who lived under the shade of mutual love,— considerate one of another. I was privileged to mark,— not only to mark the ripening graces of the aged, but also the rich young verdure and fruitfulness of many young converts to Christ; and to me it is like a return to the first year of my youthful ministry,— when I can look around me and see my children grown now to man and womanhood, walking in the truth, and their children and grandchildren following in their fathers' foot-prints. A blessed testimony this to the faithfulness and truth of the God of the covenant. "Instead of thy fathers shall be thy children, whom thou shalt make princes in all the earth."

My heart goes back with gratitude and loving regard to the past, and looks forward with hope and longing desire to even the still more enlarged and brighter visions of devoted lives, and sanctified endowments that loom even now out of the mists of the coming years. The buds are on the spray; the blossoms shall ere long open, and the beautiful coloring of God's gracious hand shall show itself ere long on the sheaves that angels' hands shall gather into His garner on His great harvest-day.

May the good Lord continue to bless you, and His holy word continue among you, and take to himself all the glory. Amen and amen.

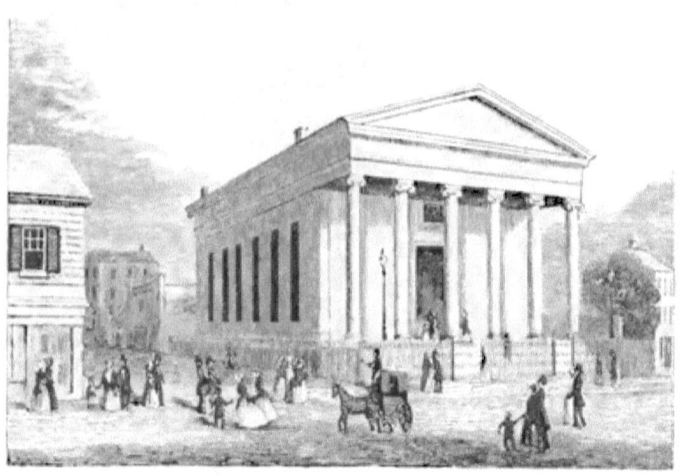

The Church at the Corner of Grand and Crosby Streets.

Historical Sermon

BY THE

Rev. Joseph R. Kerr, D. D., Pastor.

Remember the days of old, consider the years of generation and generation.—Deut. xxxii. 7.

THESE words are found in the famous song of Moses, a song which sweeps through his Farewell to Israel like a grand national epic strewn with such high thoughts and sublime conceptions as entitle it to be ranked amongst the noblest specimens of poetry in ancient or modern literature.

It is as full of trust for the future as of gratitude for the past, but the impassioned part of it seems to have been inspired largely by the days and the years that were gone.

And this is reasonable; for who can view tomorrow as he views yesterday? We seekers after revelation may be looking too long in the wrong direction when we keep our eyes only in front. The vision of new things is ever hazy, while the vision of old things may be clear and cheering as they are reviewed in the light of retrospect and amid the gracious dealings of a covenant God.

It is therefore not so much the "hereafter" as the "hitherto" which prompts our psalm to-day, and moves us to build with wayside stones the memorial of a vanished century.

When this church-century began, the Revolutionary war was closed. The independence of the colonies was a recognized fact, but there remained yet to be accomplished the organization and development of the Republic. As the enthusiasm of success began to subside, the exhaustion and sacrifice of the struggle became known and felt, so that between 1783 and 1789 was one of the most trying periods of our early national history.

The city of New-York was then in its infancy. It had experienced the hardships of the war, but, with its natural buoyancy and great commercial instinct, was already stirring with thrift and growing with the new life.

Churches had been organized, and church-edifices erected by the Reformed Dutch, the Episcopalians, and the Presbyterians; while a Society of Friends and a Jewish congregation were also in existence.

The Presbyterians had two churches,—the First, which was founded in 1716; and the Scotch, which was formed in 1756. The First occupied two places of worship, one on Wall street, near Broadway, where the Rev. Dr. John Rogers ministered, and the other at the corner of Beekman and Nassau streets, with the Rev. James Wilson in its pulpit, as the colleague of Dr. Rogers. The Scotch Presbyterian Church was on Cedar street, near Broadway, and its minister was the accomplished and beloved Dr. John Mason. It was then known as the "First Associate Reformed Church in New-York."

The "Associate Reformed" denomination was the result of a union of two bodies, which originated in secessions from the Established Church of Scotland. This union was not as complete as the hearts of its promoters had hoped. Indeed, it had not been accepted at all by some parties who, after making a formal protest and entering an appeal to the Synod in Scotland, refused their fellowship, declaring that they considered themselves, on good grounds, to be the true Associate Presbytery, with all the powers thereof inhering to them.

By these distractions and divisions, the cause of the Associate Church was brought very low, and an account of the situation, with a petition for help, was sent over to the mother country. The Synod unanimously approved of the course taken by the protestants, and resolved to send the asked-for help without delay.

In the summer of 1784, Mr. John Foster, a ruling elder in the Associate Church at Salem, New-York, wrote a letter to the Rev. William Marshall, in Philadelphia, Pa., who had been foremost in refusing to abide by the union which had taken place.

This letter speaks of the circumstances of the friends of the Secession cause in New-York, and asks for information concerning the affairs and prospects of the Presbytery of Pennsylvania.

Mr. Marshall, although replying with an evident feeling of solicitude and a sense of discouragement, rejoices at the same time in the fact that there were those in America who were standing firm by their convictions of truth and duty.

Then, as a bit of news, he says: "Last fall, a probationer arrived from Scotland for our help, who is pious, learned, sensible, but of a weak voice; this spring, the Synod has sent us an actual member, possessed of every gracious and acquired qualification suited to this country." That licentiate afterward became the distinguished Dr. Anderson, and the other was a young minister who had been granted ordination, with the special view of his crossing the Atlantic to help on the work here; and he was the Rev. Thomas Beveridge, the founder, but not the first pastor, of this our belóved church.

The letter of Mr. Marshall, already quoted from, concludes with this suggestion: "I think the friends of Christ with you should form themselves into a praying society; that you should be much employed in representing the cause of God at His throne; that you should be steady, pointed, and consistent in your profession."

The date of this was July 15, 1784; but there is a paper bearing the date of July 15, 1779, which embodies the precise idea suggested by Mr. Marshall. This document is in the form of a covenant, drawn up and signed by

JOHN McFARLAND,   JOHN McALLISTER,
GEORGE GOSMAN,   ANDREW WRIGHT, and
JAMES CRAIG,   ROBERT GOSMAN.

The original draft is still preserved, and is, in its way, a curiosity as well as a treasure. It is distinguished by strong religious fervor, admirable discernment, and much practical wisdom.

By this covenant these six godly men formed themselves into a praying society, which convened at stated times in private houses, for social worship, growing slowly in numbers and graciously in usefulness, until the arrival of the Rev. Mr. Beveridge in the spring of 1785. He had been laboring throughout the previous winter in Pennsylvania, also in various parts of the State of New-York, and finally, being sent to this city, he found this praying society ready to be organized into a church; and, the way being clear, he proceeded, in due time, to constitute the "First Associate Presbyterian Church of New-York City," remaining with it as stated supply for four or five years, doing good service, and greatly beloved by all the people.

The act of incorporation does not appear until the year 1803, when Peter Fenton, Samuel Milligan, William Robertson, George Cleland, John MacFarlane, and John McKee were duly elected trustees. The records show, however, that in 1787 ground was purchased on Nassau street, near Maiden Lane, and a church edifice was erected upon it for the uses of the Society. This was while Mr. Beveridge was supplying the pulpit. The lot cost two hundred and fifty pounds, and the building three hundred and fifty pounds, all of which was in a short time subscribed and paid. The property was held in private names, there being as yet no incorporation.

The church was a small frame structure, severely plain as to its exterior, having a window on each side of the front door, no vestibule within, and but two ranges of cushionless pews on either side of a narrow aisle that led from the door to the pulpit. The floor was sanded, and candles in tin sockets hung around the walls whenever an evening service was held.

In the oldest Record Book that I have been able to reach there is a long list of " subscribers," but to what or for what purpose is not stated. It is probable that some of the money went to the building fund of this first church on Nassau street, and also to the usual church expenses of later years. Evidently the pew-rentals would not of themselves furnish sufficient income, and hence regular subscriptions were added.

In the August of 1789 Mr. Beveridge accepted a call from Cambridge, N. Y., in which charge he continued until his death in 1798. He was a man eminent for personal piety, and he was " much countenanced in his ministry." His ashes lie in Barnet church-yard, and his biographer writes, " Few in this age possess an equal assemblage of gifts and graces, with as few imperfections." After Mr. Beveridge's retirement from this pulpit, it was supplied for nearly three years by ministers either sent from neighboring congregations, or who, happening to be in town, were glad to serve it on the Sabbath ; and it was not until October 12, 1792, that the first pastor was ordained and installed in the person of the Rev. John Cree. Mr. Beveridge presided on the occasion and preached the sermon from 2d Timothy, ii. 2, "The same commit thou to faithful men, who shall be able to teach others."

The afternoon and evening of this day were spent by the members of the Associate Presbytery, together with the elders and other members of this church, in solemn humiliation and prayer, after which they all with uplifted hands entered into what was called The Solemn Engagement to Duties.

It is to be regretted that we have neither the names nor the number of these early officers and members, and that we are without any particulars of the pastorate thus formed, save that it extended over only two years, when it was terminated by the removal of Mr. Cree to Ligonier, in Pennsylvania, where he died.

During the subsequent eight years there was no pastoral settlement. It was at a period in the history of the Associate Church in America when ministers and preachers were not abundant, and all the available force was in demand for apostolic work in planting and strengthening congregations over the country;—here, in part at least, may be the explanation of this very long interval. In it, however, the people enjoyed the ministrations of some superior and well-known men. Among these was the Rev. William Marshall, the writer of the letter from which quotation has been made, and the leader in the opposition to the union between the Associate and Reformed Churches, a man full of conscience and zeal for the truth as he saw it; also, the Rev. David Goodwillie, of blessed memory and extensive usefulness, whose earnest piety, sound judgment, and cheerful disposition made him a benediction to all who knew him and who sat under his preaching; also, the Rev. Francis Pringle, who was afterward settled for thirty years in Carlisle, Pa. He occupied our pulpit for the entire winter following the summer of 1799, and his work was so rich and strong that many in the congregation began to think of him in connection with the pastorate.

But before anything was done in this direction, the Rev. Thomas Hamilton was sent by the Presbytery of Pennsylvania to minister to the church for a few Sabbaths. He was a native of Washington County, Pa., where his father was a highly respected citizen and at one time in the shrievalty. His mother was a devoted Christian, and her touch visibly molded the youth's future. He graduated at Dickenson College, studied theology under the Rev. Dr. Anderson, and was licensed to preach about the year 1801. When he came here the church was ripe for settlement, and the impression made by him was so favorable that in a short time he received a call to be its pastor, which he accepted, being ordained and installed in the summer of 1802.

Thus ended that long interval of eight years —years of fidelity and perseverance on the part of the Lord's people, many of whom cannot be identified at this late day, but whose names are written in heaven.

Under the ministry of Mr. Hamilton the little church became too small, therefore a larger and more pretentious frame structure was erected, partly on the site of the old building and partly on ground adjoining, which was leased from the Dutch Church.

While the new edifice was going up, the regular services were held in a neighboring room, at the corner of William and Fulton streets, probably occupying the site of what is now so widely known as the Fulton Street Prayer Meeting.

Let this fact go indelibly into the record, for who can tell how much this old covenant and praying society of ours has had to do with making that locality such a stair-way of holy light and peace to the wandering and the weary!

With pleasant church accommodations; with a roll increased in numbers and wealth; with its pulpit filled by a cultivated, spiritual, and zealous minister; without a penny of indebtedness; with generally prevailing harmony, — sixteen happy years came and went. God had once more proved himself the hearer and the answerer of prayer.

But at the expiration of this time disease attacked the beloved Hamilton, and in the month of August, 1818, he resigned his church and his spirit into the hands of God, dying just in his prime, just when the Lord's pleasure was prospering most by his labors. He left a widow, two sons, and a daughter to mourn his departure, in company with an afflicted congregation and a saddened community.

The pulpit, thus made vacant, remained so for four years, when it was filled by the calling of the Rev. Andrew Stark, D. D., a native of the parish of Slamanan, in the county of Sterling, Scotland, a graduate of the University of Glasgow, and honored with the degree of Doctor of Laws by the University of London. He was a man well versed in the Scriptures, of strong convictions concerning the truths of revealed religion, and unusually wise in winning souls. Exactness and punctuality were among his leading characteristics. His coming to be Mr. Hamilton's successor proved highly favorable to the prosperity of the church, healing some divisions which had sprung up, and increasing its power for good in many directions.

He had about him, in the ruling eldership, such men as the Pattersons, Wrights, McFarlane, Fenton, Geery, Clendenning, Edwards, Highet, McNab, Miller, Irwin, Boyd, Chalmers, John Duncan, William Whitewright, and Edward Mackenzie; while in the congregation were such rising and influential men as John Aitken, David Morrison, Joseph and James Stuart, and others with them who followed his leadership into much that concerned the life of the church. Of course, now and then there were differences in views, and in some cases decided independence of action, but Dr. Stark was always able to guide and decide, so that the integrity of his work kept on, unbroken and blessed.

In May, 1822, and two years after his installation, the congregation resolved to change the location of the church, and move up-town. The property on Nassau street was sold, and lots were purchased on the corner of Grand and Mercer streets, where a good brick edifice was erected, which was first occupied in August, 1824. The cost, including the site, was about $14,000.

This pastorate lasted for twenty-six years,— the longest in the history of the church,— and represents more than a quarter of a century of precious Christian life and power.

In the year 1830, a colony went out to form a

new organization, and, under the care of the Rev. James Irving as the first pastor, established itself in a new building at the corner of Thompson and Prince streets. Mr. Irving died after only four years of service, and was succeeded in the pastorate by the well-known and greathearted Hugh Henry Blair. But the new venture was embarrassed with debt, the house of worship had to be sold under foreclosure, disagreements arose among the membership, until at last the church divided, and the part of it that retained its original name, "The Second Associate Church," after removing several times to other places and remaining for a season without a pastor, at last secured the Rev. William J. Cleland, and shortly after purchased a house of worship at the corner of Houston and Forsyth streets.

The other portion of the people who adhered to Mr. Blair constituted the Third or "Charles Street Associate Church," ultimately building the substantial brick structure in which they still worship, and where the Rev. Dr. Blair labored and prospered up to the time of his death. The present pastor of the church is the Rev. James White, D. D. It appears that there were other offshoots from this parent stem, but of a less formal and distinct character than the ones just indicated; and thus the strong life of the Grand Street Church was throwing into the community from time to time healthful influences and consecrated forces for the advancement of the kingdom.

At last Dr. Stark's health began to break. Although never very robust, yet he stood up long and well under the heavy strain of his official duties, but finally had to yield to medical advice and cease temporarily from labor. He sailed for Scotland on the 3d of July, 1849, fully expecting to return in a few months and take up again his parish cares. But soon after arriving on the other side, his symptoms became more unfavorable, and his little remaining strength commenced to waste away, until the 18th of the following September, when he passed into his eternal reward at Dennyloanhead, Scotland, at the house of his cousin, the Rev. Andrew Stark, who was also a Presbyterian minister.

The tidings of his demise and the sense of its own loss plunged the church into profound distress. When the remains arrived in this city they were received with tears and every mark of affection and respect by a people who had known and prized the man and the minister for over twenty-five years. His funeral sermon was preached by the Rev. Peter Bullions, D. D., and his grave was made in Greenwood Cemetery, where surviving friends could often come to read the writing on the memorial stone and sigh for

> "The touch of a vanished hand,
> The sound of a voice that was still."

What memories are stirred by such names as Marshall, Goodwillie, Pringle, Stark, and Bullions — memories which droop like ivies across the history of the old Associate Church! Upon the present church walls are perpetuated the names and virtues of Hamilton and Stark, and so, they being dead, still speak to us whenever we are in the house of God.

After the death of Dr. Stark, the pulpit remained vacant for nearly two years, when, in 1851, a call was extended to the Rev. John Thomson, D. D., at that time minister of St. David's Church, St. John, New Brunswick.

This call was accepted, and on the 9th of June, 1851, another pastoral relationship was formed, which included all but a score of years, and that lies to-day upon our affection like an unclasped chain of gold.

About a twelvemonth from the new pastor's installation, it was decided to change again the site of the church building. At the corner of Grand and Crosby streets stood a large white marble church, remarkable for its beauty, and considered at that day one of the most elegant ecclesiastical edifices in that part of the city. It was the "Scotch Presbyterian Church," and its pastor was the Rev. Joseph McElroy, D. D., the successor of the Rev. Dr. John M. Mason and the Rev. Robert McLeod.

This society, desiring to go up to West Fourteenth street, offered its handsome property for sale, and our people buying it were given possession at the expiration of two years from the date of purchase; and with this possession they also received some valuable accessions from the membership of the other church, in those who were disinclined to follow it to the new location.

But before this removal there occurred a still more important change, affecting the name, the customs, and the life of our organization.

A restlessness had been growing on the part of some, which at last found controlling expression, in the demand for a different denominational fellowship; and upon formal application being made to the Presbytery of New-York, the church and its pastor were admitted into the communion of the Presbyterian Church of North America, on the twentieth day of June, 1853, with the name of "The Grand Street Presbyterian Church of New-York City."

Under the wise and able management of the pastor, the comfort and growth of the congregation suffered no real interruption by this transfer;

and when the marble edifice was entered, it was but to advance along the line of a gracious and lasting success. Dr. Thomson remained in charge until 1861, when he felt it to be his duty to accept a call which had been extended to him from the Knox Church, Galt, Ontario. The decision caused profound regret among his people and his friends in New-York, who found themselves unable to alter it. After his withdrawal, the pulpit was tendered to the Rev. Samuel R. Wilson, D. D., now of Louisville, Kentucky, who came to it just before the opening of our Civil War. Those days were full of trembling anxieties, and as the conflict burst and raged, both Church and State were searched as by fire.

It was a most unfavorable time in which to begin a new pastorate, but Dr. Wilson took hold with energy, and endeavored to carry on the Lord's work as it had fallen to him. With a vigorous mind and much power as a public speaker, he soon made himself felt, but the great political excitements, and the distractions in commercial and social life, were so disturbing and confusing that he seems to have become discouraged, and we find him tendering his resignation and retiring from the pulpit in February, 1863.

But it must be said, and here is the place to say it, that the loyalty and patriotism of this church throughout that long national crisis were of the stanchest and noblest character. It was no neutral camp; its sympathy with the rightful government was anything but lukewarm. It had no patience with secession; its prayers, its money, and its blood were ever ready for the defense and preservation of the Union.

That struggle is now far past, and it is delightful to observe how the scars are growing out like the letters in the bark as the tree thickens and spreads; but we cannot forget, and we ought not to forget in this era of forgiveness and restored confidence, who stood fast and strong by the national standard in the hour of its greatest peril.

It was not long after Dr. Wilson's withdrawal that the thoughts and affections of the people turned once more toward their former pastor, the Rev. Dr. Thomson, who was rendering good service in Galt, Ontario.

The appeal for his return was so hearty and unanimous that he could not put it aside, and he was soon installed a second time over a church of which he had every reason to be proud, and that rallied again about him with the old enthusiasm and success.

Four years after this reunion another change of location was agreed upon. The city was rapidly pushing northwards, the pressure of business was converting residences into offices and stores, and business men were locating their homes in the upper wards. It was therefore thought best to exchange Grand street for West Thirty-fourth street, although the latter was considered to be then in the outskirts of the town.

The corner-stone of the present edifice was laid July 7th, 1866, in the presence of a large assembly, composed of the church officers, members of the congregation and their friends, together with the teachers and children of the Sabbath-school. The ceremonies were conducted by the pastor, with the assistance of the Revs. Drs. Scott and Krebs, and the Revs. Messrs. Adams and Mingens.

The Lecture Room was ready for occupation on the 6th of May, 1867, and the entire church was finished and dedicated, free of debt, in October of the same year. The pastor was assisted in the dedication services by the Revs. W. T. Morrison and D. M. Quackenbush, and by Revs. Drs. Gardiner Spring and John Rogers. The cost of the building and the land was upward of $140,000.

The removal from Grand street necessitated another name for the church, and, with the permission of the Supreme Court of the State, it assumed the historic title to which by birth in the Presbyterian family of this city it was entitled.

The First Church being organized in 1716, the Scotch Church in 1756, and the Brick Church having been part of the First Church up to 1809, and so properly ranking third, we came next in order, and from that day onward have been known as the Fourth Presbyterian Church of the City of New-York.

The next important step was the planting and developing of the West Side Mission.

Toward the close of the year 1869, an Association was formed in the congregation for the originating of spheres of Christian usefulness, in which the working power of the church might be actively engaged. This society is still in vigorous existence, and is known as "The Social and Benevolent Association." Its first President was Mr. James Robertson, now a leading officer in the Regent Square Presbyterian Church of London, England, the Rev. J. Oswald Dykes, D. D., pastor. Through a special committee, West 33d street, between the Ninth and Tenth Avenues, was selected as a convenient and needy center for mission work, and a small hall over a stable was rented at the rate of $400 a year, in which a Sabbath-school was begun, and occasional preaching provided. Mr. Robertson was the first Superintendent of this school, and it must ever be greatly indebted for his zeal and generosity in its behalf. In April of 1870, Mr.

Henry C. Cronin was appointed the first missionary in charge, at a salary of $750 per annum, which was afterward increased to $1200 per annum.

Three years of self-denying effort and genuine progress were spent in this old hall, the neighborhood changing perceptibly for the better, and the accommodations becoming at last too small and inconvenient.

The building of a chapel was then undertaken, a valuable lot having been secured on the opposite side of the street.

On Sabbath evening, December 14, 1873, the new and handsome rooms were dedicated to the worship and service of God; the whole property having cost the church fully $20,000, all of which was paid. The enterprise from its inception has never had a debt to embarrass it. Its friends have been good, and the work done has been attended by the rich blessing of the Master.

Among those who were especially interested in it, and who were prompt to show it at every opportunity, was that devoted Christian man and elder, the late Mr. John Aitken. Remembering it in his will with a bequest of $5000, the Association has inscribed his name in memorial brass upon one of the chapel walls.

Mr. Cronin retired from his position as missionary in 1877, and was succeeded by the Rev.

Edward Pratt, who remained in charge until 1881, when he resigned in order to settle in the West. Mr. Pratt was followed by the Rev. Alfred Blewett, who labored until 1883, when he went to a neighboring charge, and the Rev. W. J. McDowell, the present incumbent, was invited to take the vacant place, which he is filling with fidelity and success.

Once and again Bible-readers have been employed to coöperate with the missionary in the cultivation of the field. The last one was personally employed by Mrs. John Aitken, who thus perpetuates and extends with her own interest the cause so dear to her lamented husband.

The Mission Sabbath-school has always been a marked feature of this work, and there have been but two Superintendents besides Mr. James Robertson,—Dr. D. H. Goodwillie, who gave much of his valuable professional time to promote its interests, and Mr. James Kydd, who is now in charge, and whose services are becoming more indispensable with each succeeding year.

The first Secretary of the school was Mr. John W. Aitken; the second and only other, Mr. John H. Allen, who still serves in this capacity with unwearied zeal and great efficiency.

No better corps of teachers has been found anywhere, and there are no better behaved or more studious pupils than those who have been and are still identified with our West Side Chapel.

In May, 1873, a Juvenile Missionary Society was formed in the school, and it is still in existence. The money collected has been devoted to missionary work mostly outside of the local field. Up to the last Report the gifts of the children in this way have amounted to $1614.11 ; and only those who have been in the homes of some of these children can appreciate how much of self-denial this means, and how loudly it speaks for the desire of the little ones to do good unto others. In addition to this they have sewing-classes, and literary and musical entertainments carried through by themselves under proper direction.

This enterprise may well distinguish the second part of Dr. Thomson's pastorate. He it was who called the meeting for the formation of the Association, and by his sympathy and encouragement, with the aid of such men as Joseph and James Stuart, John Aitken, James and David Morrison, and others, carried it prosperously into the permanent building and toward an assured future.

His and their policy was evidently an aggressive one; the fine position on Thirty-fourth street was not to be a place of selfish ease or narrow ideas. The congregation had come up-town to spend and be spent for Christ.

In the ruling eldership of this second term the pastor had with him James Stuart, John Aitken, John Kirkpatrick, William Dalrymple, Alexander Edwards, James Allen, John Morrison, Dr. Edward F. Parsons, Samuel Kydd, James Morrison, James Robertson, Frederick Blume, John Strachan, Joseph A. Macdonald, Archibald McLintock, James Kydd, and John Iverach, elected and ordained in groups at different dates. And along with these was a company of men and women who were truly fellow-helpers in every good word and work.

Will it be deemed invidious if Joseph Stuart is named again, and Robert Marshall and David Morrison and William Eagle?

The last three are still alive, and Mr. Morrison, although advanced in age, holds the presidency of our Board of Trustees with the grace and usefulness of a much younger man.

And then there are other names which link both the ministries of Dr. Stark and Dr. Thomson in one long term of membership and fellowship: Charters, Warnock, Bryson, McCrea, Scott, Hutton, Elder, Legget, McClellan, Chalmers, Cameron, McGay, Little, Harrison, Dinwiddie; and there are others yet which represent warm friendship and personal comfort to Dr. Thomson in the closing years of his service: Taylor, Craig, Nicholson, Robert Allan, A. M. Stewart, Turnbull, McIntire, Anderson — and the list is not yet exhausted!

When, in 1875, by reason of personal and family ill health, Dr. Thomson felt compelled to ask once again for a dissolution of the pastoral relation, his request was only acceded to because it seemed imperative that he should have an entire and protracted rest from all official care.

He left the church strong and united, free from debt, and well furnished to fill a yet larger place in the metropolis of the nation.

One of the benedictions of this centennial season is in having him and his daughter present with us all the way from the manse beyond the sea. And it is a privilege to say to him that in the time to come, as in the time that is past, the prayers and affection of this church for him and his will be as the night stars which shine upon the Grampians, and as the heather when it blossoms beside his door.

The pulpit, being once more vacant, was tendered to the present pastor, then of Philadelphia, Pa., and in charge of the North United Presbyterian Church of that city. It becomes him only to say that ten years have come and gone since that November invitation was accepted. Coming together as total strangers, believing that the Great Head of the Church called us in His providence, it was very much like an oriental wedding, where the contracting parties never see each other until the nuptial day. We have wept and rejoiced together; we have worked and rested together; we have lost and won together; and it is but right that we should together attest the fact that the Lord God has been with us as He was with our fathers, and that He keeps His covenant unto all generations.

And now permit me to rapidly sketch some of our more prominent organizations and societies, in addition to the one already noticed in connection with the chapel.

At a meeting held in the church, June 28, 1827, Alexander Christie, John Edwards, and others agreed to form themselves into a society, and to invite the coöperation of their brethren, for the purpose of organizing a Sabbath-school in connection with the congregation.

A committee was appointed, with the Rev. Dr. Stark as chairman, to prepare a constitution for the regulation of the school, and the constitution presented and adopted at that time remains the law of our present Morning Sabbath-school Association.

Messrs. Middlemas, Highet, Paterson, and Smith interested themselves deeply in this effort in behalf of the young.

Religious instruction had previously been given to the youth of the church on week days, by means of catechism classes held in the houses, and conducted partly by godly women, who thus aided the parents in caring for the spiritual welfare of their children; but now it was proposed to open a school on the Lord's Day in the church for regular Bible and catechetical study. The first officers and teachers were: Mr. John Highet, superintendent; Miss Catherine Wood, assistant superintendent; John Patterson, secretary. Male teachers: Messrs. Christie, John Edwards, William and John Smith, James McNab, and Thomas Dennistown; female teachers: Misses Eliza and Mary Smith, Ferguson, McCready, Welsh, Stoddart, and McClure.

It was early resolved that the lessons should be uniform, and, from the very first, meetings of the teachers were held for prayer and preparation for the work of teaching. In addition to these, there were meetings of a more general character, at which papers upon Sabbath-school interests and claims were read and discussed.

The visitation of the scholars at their residences was not neglected, special committees being appointed for this purpose. Nor was the pleasure of the children overlooked; and the first entertainment offered to them seems to have been a visit to the Mechanics' Institute at Castle Garden in 1836.

In 1828, a Sabbath-school Library was opened, and formed an important help in imparting religious instruction. Only the best literature was admitted to its shelves, and the use of it was freely allowed to the members of the congregation as well as to the pupils,— a privilege continued unto this day.

In 1844, a Sabbath-school Missionary Society was organized, and a missionary spirit has been a feature in the work, as carried on by different hands. Especial interest has been manifested for helping to establish schools in the southern and western sections of our land, while the cause of Foreign Missions has become a part of the yearly thought and provision, especially since the Rev. William T. Morrison, son of Elder John Morrison, prepared himself here for work among the Chinese, and subsequently educated a class of Chinese boys, who were supported during their course by this school and members of this church.

Of these youth, two were converted, and one, entering the ministry, has for a long time been an earnest preacher of the gospel among his own countrymen. He is a member of the Presbytery of Ning Po, is pastor of two native churches, and has interested the school in a Presbyterial Academy at Ning Po, at which two of his own sons have graduated, and where some of the students are professing and praying members of the Christian church.

Then something was done in the way of aiding to establish the first Sabbath-school in the city of

Rome, and contributions have gone from time to time into the treasuries of the Waldensian churches as their needs were presented.

This old and honored school has had fourteen superintendents — John Highet, John Miller, David Irwin, William Boyd, Humphreys Miller, Robert McClellan, Alexander Edwards, Sylvester Patullo, John Aitken, Dr. Edward F. Parsons, D. C. Tiebout, James Kydd, the Rev. Dr. Thomson; and Frederick Blume, who has been faithfully and ably discharging the duties of his office for the past thirteen years.

The longest term is that of Mr. John Aitken, who aggregated twenty-two and a half years. He was exceedingly fond of the young, and that fondness was most heartily reciprocated. So he was kept in leadership for all that long period; and more than once when he actually retired, it was only to be reinstated by the appreciation of his fellow-workers and the earnest wishes of the children themselves.

On this noble roll blazes the name of Sylvester Patullo, who was Superintendent for only eighteen months, and who died in England, June 7, 1856. He was a man of special gifts and with such a rapture in his faith that he was literally a burning and shining light amongst old and young.

A third school in connection with the church was organized on the 17th of April, 1876, and its sessions appointed for the afternoon of every Lord's Day.

This appeared to be needed because many of the youth who attended the morning school were going elsewhere in the afternoons for their instructions and fellowships. While the chapel was open at that part of the day, and its teachers ready to welcome all who might attend, yet it was a fact that quite a number of our children did not go there; and so this new provision was made for them at home.

The result has more than justified the experiment, and from the opening day until now this school has flourished. It is not a duplicate of the older ones; it has its own officers and teachers, its own tastes, its own methods, and its own life. This, of itself, creates for it a special place without interfering with the fields of the other two.

The first Superintendent was Andrew Little, so long and prominently identified with our church. He gave the best attention to his office until warned by failing strength that he must stop. The next was Joseph G. Harrison, whose generous life has been in and of us all, and whose terms of service were valuable and honorable to the end.

Elder John Macdonald came next, conscientious in the routine duties of his position; he also greatly stimulated the missionary spirit in the school.

Thomas M. Stewart is the present Superintendent, a former Vice-President of the Brooklyn Sabbath-school Association, and trained in his knowledge of the interests and wants of the young.

Associated with him, as Vice-Superintendent, is James R. Cuming, a man in whom the heart of his pastor trusts, and whose care of the Young Men's Bible Class is as tender as it is gracious.

The teaching staff is earnest and devoted, and while lately afflicted in the death of one of its brightest ornaments, it has been cheered by seeing the vacant chair filled by one who was as dear to the dead as she is an inspiration to the living.

The number of children and young people in attendance upon these schools, as reported to the last Assembly, is between four and five hundred, and usually there are more classes than teachers.

It must surely be that great and constant blessings shall come forth upon that church which looks properly after the rising generation. And we have learned since those early catechetical meetings and the founding of our first church-school that heaven's sweetest dew-fall is upon the faces of those who watch for the morning!

The Rev. David McC. Quackenbush, of the Reformed (Dutch) Church, Yorkville, and the Rev. John Reid, the successful pastor of the First

Presbyterian Church, Yonkers, had their early religious training in our communion. There are others, baptized at this font, who have become prominent in merchantry and trade, who have reached high positions in their chosen professions, whose success in life reflects in luster the godly training and religious knowledge furnished within these walls.

And it is a pleasant fact in connection with members of the old families still surviving, and also with many of their children and children's children, that this church holds the deepest place in their hearts as a spiritual home. The local attachment is as remarkable as it is beautiful, and I think it argues for the long, faithful care of the church for its households "in generation and generation."

The oldest society in connection with us is known as "The Benevolent Society." It was organized in 1795 for the purpose of relieving the poor, assisting the needy and distressed in the congregation.

The old Minute Book furnishes some curious reading, and amid all the quaintness there is the glow of a fervent charity. In the opening pages there is notice of a grant of ten pounds toward the support of two ministers lately come from Scotland and on their way to Nova Scotia. And there were other ministers with their families assisted out of this treasury,—for the country was new and the times were not always prosperous. Case after case of need is briefly noted and marked as relieved, while at nearly every meeting of the Society the dues of members were received and acknowledged.

The first president was Samuel Milligan, the first treasurer was John Scotland, and the secretary was George Thomson. The initiation fees collected at the first meeting amounted to £22 12s. 6d.

It is impossible to estimate all the money which has gone through this channel during the past ninety years; but the stream was steady and strong, for it came of a spirit that grew not weary in well-doing. The Society is still in active existence, and has a full treasury.

Next in age comes "The Ladies' City Mission Society," which was organized in 1824 as an auxiliary to the American Tract Society, with Miss Warnock and Miss Wright as managers.

The work was shortly after changed to providing clothing for poor students who were preparing for the ministry under the instruction of the Rev. Dr. Banks, in the city of Philadelphia. In 1852 the Society began to contribute for the support of the gospel in various places by aiding feeble churches and by donations to the missionary fund of the Synod. It also agreed to pay a certain amount to the "New-York City Tract Society" for the support of a missionary in the Fourteenth Ward. This last arrangement continued until 1870, since which time the Society has given annually out of its funds $500 toward the support of our West Side Chapel.

In 1866 its name was changed to that of "The Ladies' City Mission of the Fourth Presbyterian Church." This identified it fully with the church, and its auxiliary character ceased.

It has been greatly indebted to the kindness and liberality of Mr. David Irwin, who at different times donated sums of money, amounting in all to $5000, the interest of which is applied to the aid and furtherance of the Society's work. It has also been remembered with legacies by other friends who knew of its aims and rejoiced in its endeavors. Its great object from the beginning until now has been the advancement of Christ's cause among the careless and churchless multitude, and it has reason to hope that during the sixty years of its existence as a society the favor of Heaven has rested upon its efforts to the winning of many souls.

The next society to be formed was "The Bible Society," which was organized June 14, 1843, for the distribution of God's word, particularly in this city. It is an auxiliary to the New-York Bible Society, and at its annual meetings has reports and addresses showing the progress and needs of the work in a great seething community like our own.

The first officers were, the Rev. Andrew Stark, D. D., President; William Boyd, Vice-President; J. F. Clarkson, Secretary, and David Morrison, Treasurer. The money collected and paid over by this society since its formation aggregates $6130.04, and there is a small balance to-day in the treasury.

"The Ladies' Sewing Society" was formed in 1860, having for its object the providing of suitable clothing for the poor of the church and the chapel, and also the assistance of needy missionaries and their families in this and other lands. Although death and removal have made many changes in this circle, there are a few of the original members still present to unite with others in keeping up the weekly meetings, which are held throughout the winter season. Parcels and boxes are constantly being made up and sent out by these faithful women, and their generous diligence is not without its rewards.

"The Social and Benevolent Association" has already been referred to in connection with the inauguration and development of the chapel enterprise.

It is wholly distinct from the old Benevolent Society, and confines itself to the mission needs and calls as well as the partial support of the minister at the chapel. In addition to this it holds sociables in the lecture-room every few months, where the members of the church can meet together for agreeable fellowship and entertainment, and where strangers may be introduced and made welcome among us.

"The Silver Link Society" was organized November 1, 1878, and is composed entirely of young ladies, who meet from week to week for missionary and benevolent purposes, Mrs. Joseph R. Kerr being the permanent Superintendent. Although in formal connection with the Woman's Board of Missions of the Presbyterian Church, and a contributor to that important agency, this society engages also in much outside work, and sends annual donations to the McAll mission in Paris, under the care of the Rev. W. W. Newell, Jr., and to the Home of the Friendless in this city.

It has also furnished two ship-libraries through the American Seaman's Friend Society, purchased a scholarship in Hamadan, and supports a Bible reader in Petchaburi, Siam. The first officers were Miss Harrison (now Mrs. Dr. Edward Parsons), President; Miss Valentine, Vice-President; Miss Ritchie, Treasurer, and Miss Mattison, Secretary.

The active membership numbers twenty-eight and there is a good list of honorary members.

In May, 1885, the young ladies organized a branch with the name of "Pansy." The age for membership is from four to fourteen years; and its present membership is twenty-three.

This is but a glimpse at some of the ways by which this old church is trying to fulfill its mission in the world.

Its financial record has been clean and bright. Such men as Joseph and James Stuart were exceedingly jealous of its honor, and by their wise counsel and liberal deeds, seconded by others in the church, debt has never lain upon the roof, and every obligation has been met honestly and fully.

The income during the first year of its existence was £51 2s. 1d., and the expenditure about £1 less than that amount. Over $720,000 have been collected and paid out for various church and benevolent purposes, and this does not include many handsome gifts from leading members to local and public charities — gifts of which there is no trace upon our books.

The present membership is a little over 450 on the Active Roll. There are many more names on the Reserved Roll, of those who have dropped away from our sight and of whose decease we have not heard.

The Session is a model of harmony, canvassing the congregation with the pastor once every year, and frequently taking part with him in every form of church work. The present members are Archibald McLintock, Frederick Blume, Joseph A. Macdonald, James R. Cuming, John MacDonald, James Kydd, and Henry C. Smith.

The Board of Trustees is composed of David Morrison, Francis Pringle, Joseph G. Harrison, John Cameron, John H. Allen, and Marcus B. Bookstaver; and in the execution of their trusts these wear worthily the mantle of the fathers.

Throughout the church there continues to be a spirit of mutual confidence and fraternal regard; the ordinances are well attended, especially when it is remembered that the people are very much scattered; and on the days in which the Lord's Supper is dispensed, there is a gathering from even remote places, as if all wanted to be together when the blessed King comes in to see his guests.

But as the years pass familiar faces are missed, for God is calling the household one by one into His heavenly presence.

A ruling elder, Alexander Mackenzie, a good man, full of faith and of the Holy Ghost, went from us only last month. He expected to have been here to participate on this occasion, but God had provided some better thing for him. Other precious graves we have had to make this autumn; one, that of Joseph A. Macdonald, Jr., a bright lad of only sixteen summers. And there are those yet with us who are beginning to walk slowly under the weight of years, while the end of the pilgrimage is almost in sight. But their faith fails not, their hope grows brighter as the shadows fall, and their tones are soft and tender as we bend our heads for their evening blessing. Among these is one greatly beloved whose ministerial life has been long and rich; whose ripe experience and wise counsels are always ours for the asking; whose hymns we sing to-day; and whose "good gray head" seems to carry, not the snows of his eighty-five winters, but the dawnlight of a happy eternity. May the Lord God of our fathers keep and bless us every one! I cannot call every one, but He knows us all, just as He remembers those names that have faded out under the rain and moss of the departed century.

It but remains for me to repeat the expression of the profound and adoring gratitude with which we recognize the good hand of our God upon us in all the days that are gone; and then to voice our united entreaty that He would continue to have respect unto "the covenant," hear and answer our prayers, making us a name and a praise unto all generations. And to Him shall be the glory for His loving mercy and for His truth's sake. Amen and amen.

Monday, October 26, 1885.—7.30 P. M.

Addresses by the

Rev. William Ormiston, D. D., LL. D.

Rev. Howard Crosby, D. D., LL. D.

Rev. John Hall, D. D., LL. D.

The Rev. John Thomson, D. D., presided, and was assisted by the Rev. Henry J. Van Dyke, Jr., D. D.

ADDRESS

BY THE

REV. WILLIAM ORMISTON, D. D., LL. D.

IT affords me unspeakable pleasure to be present on this occasion of Christian rejoicing, on many accounts, and first of all, that I can see you, Mr. Chairman, in your venerability and freshness, with eye undimmed and strength unabated, sitting, presiding over the present gathering, surrounded, as you are, by your former parishioners and friends of other years. And it must be peculiarly gratifying, I think, to meet with them, many of whom you have guided and admitted to the fellowship of the Christian church; whose nuptial vows you have consecrated and blessed; whose deepest sorrows you have sympathized with, and by the death-bed of many of whose friends you have ministered consolation. It is almost an enviable position for you to have tonight, and I congratulate you upon it very much, and especially when all the memories of other days are likely to be evoked, and all the bonds of Christian fellowship brightened and strengthened, and the hopes of future fellowship joyously assured. I congratulate, also, the congregation on the completion of a century of church life, and on all the manifest tokens of the divine favor which have rested on them during more than three generations. The pillar of cloud by day and of fire by night has hovered over you to direct your way, and whether by the bitter waters of Mara, or the green palm trees and crystal fountains of Elim, whether on the mount or in the valley, the promised presence has been ever with you, and the daily manna has not failed to fall around your tents. To-day you are in the land of corn and wine; your blessings greatly abound; your candle burns brightly, and your hearts rejoice, and you are prepared to say, "The Lord has done great things for us, whereof we are glad"; and we that are here to-night rejoicing with you can gratefully and joyously in Christian sympathy say, "Truly, the Lord hath done great things for you."

I greet you right heartily in my own name, but I rejoice especially in the privilege and high honor of bringing to you the joyous greetings and sincere congratulations of the church I represent, the Reformed Church of America, your oldest sister church in this land, one with you in doctrine and discipline, and in the earnest maintenance of Christ's crown and covenant; and bring you the hearty greetings, in addition, of the Collegiate Reformed Dutch Church of the City of New-York, the oldest Protestant church in America, so far as I know. Through one of her youngest sons by her kindly adoption, she sends you her, not to say sisterly, or even motherly, but I may say grandmotherly salutations. A hundred years is a respectable age for a maiden church, and certainly furnishes ground for high hopes of matronly usefulness and housewifely service in after days. But seven years ago we celebrated, not our centennial, but quarter-millennial anniversary, at which some of you were present. When your church was organized in 1785, the then venerable Collegiate Church had attained its hundred and fifty-seventh year, and she has watched with kind and sisterly affection over your cradle, your infancy, your girlhood, and your maturity; and once again most happily I greet you on what may be regarded as the period of your attaining your majority. The Collegiate Church, the oldest congregation in the city, wishes you all prosperity and abundant usefulness, and expresses the hope that your noble achievements in the past may be only an earnest of your greater and more extended successes in the future. Your peace and prosperity are our joy. We rejoice with you. And as you have once already changed your ecclesiastical relations, should you at any time, for any reason, wish to make another change, we extend to you the arms of cordial welcome and are ready to receive you; but be assured there is no feeling of jealousy or envy, or anything else than that of zealous coöperation in accomplishing the work which in common has been assigned us to do. Whatever cheers you shall gladden us, and whatever tries or grieves you will surely sadden us. We will joy and rejoice with you as we do to-day when things go well with you, and we will weep with you if a time of trial or adversity should overtake you.

I congratulate you upon the facts of your past history, and upon the succession of able, gifted, zealous, godly men who have ministered unto you, from the earnest, devout, and saintly Beveridge, who organized the congregation and supplied its pulpit for six or eight years, to the genial, brilliant, eloquent, and effective preacher, and assiduous and sympathetic pastor, my highly esteemed and truly beloved brother, Dr. Kerr, who is not more acceptable to you, his people, as a pastor, by reason of his eminent gifts and great diligence and obvious success, than he is endeared to, and esteemed by, his brethren in the ministry for his unaffected simplicity and the true manliness of his character, as well as the affability and courtesy of his manners.

The first pastor of this church, Mr. Cree, had a very brief pastorate, and soon passed away. After an interval of some years, Mr. Hamilton came, and left his impress on the young congregation, rendering faithful service for some sixteen years, greatly beloved. His memory dear is fresh with some of the elder members still. Then came Mr. Stark, a man of iron will, of strong and vigorous intellect and determined purpose, whose ministry covered a period of more than a quarter of a century. During his pastorate, the congregation moved from Nassau street to Grand. These men have passed away to their rest and their reward.

In 1851 the honored guest of the congregation and chairman of this meeting took charge of the congregation, and soon after his coming, the congregation, which had hitherto been connected with the associate body of Scotch Presbyterians, united with the great Presbyterian body, a change which has been found advantageous and is now loyally maintained. It was in 1858 that I first heard Dr. Thomson in his church in Grand street. I was a stranger to him then; shortly afterward, however, I made his acquaintance on a visit to a dear common friend, now at rest, on the banks of the Hudson — a visit peculiarly rich to me as the beginning of life-long friendships, and of very warm and tender memories. And ever since that time, both in Canada, where Dr. Thomson labored for a time, and in New-York, I have had frequent fellowship with him. Long may he be spared to serve the Master and the church in the land of his nativity and mine; though I hope he will pardon me if I say I wish he had remained here, and even if he had gone home, that he had not given his adherence to the theory of the State Church. He did not always like it any better than I do, to my certain knowledge.

With the present pastor my intercourse has been most intimate, and very delightful and refreshing. He is a brother of the heart. We have not only frequently exchanged pulpits, but mutual affection and sympathy and brotherhood as well. May his pastorate be extended till it shall far exceed that of his predecessors, and until his raven locks shall rival even yours, my dear sir (turning to Dr. Thomson), in snowy and venerable whiteness.

I am personally acquainted, also, with not a few of the families in this congregation, and therefore I can rejoice all the more heartily with them. I always feel myself perfectly at home in their pulpit or by the ingle-sides in their homes.

I congratulate you still further upon the peace and harmony that now exists so largely among you. May it ever continue, till every heart and home shall beat as that of one man, and its fruits abound to your enlargement and usefulness.

I congratulate you still further on the large increase of your membership during these last years, and on the amount of missionary work which you have done in aiding evangelistic work in this great city.

And now, on entering the second century of your existence as a church, may you receive a fresh baptism from on high, and pastor and people alike rejoice in a time of great refreshing from the presence of the Lord. May you so build that your work will remain, and when another century shall have passed by, which it is not at all likely any of us will live to see, your descendants shall have abundant reason to give God thanks for the noble ancestry whence they have sprung. May this beautiful house stand till then, a memorial of your love and zeal, and be even more hallowed than now as the birthplace of thousands of souls, and by the accumulated associations of seasons of felt communion with each other and fellowship with the Father and with His Son.

I gather up all the hearts of my congregation and put them into one single hearty congratulation and good wish for your present joy, your future prosperity, and your eternal felicity.

Address

BY THE

Rev. Howard Crosby, D. D., LL. D.

MR. CHAIRMAN AND DEAR CHRISTIAN FRIENDS: I do not know exactly what I represent here to-night beyond myself. I come as belonging to the great Presbyterian Church to which you belong. I cannot talk to you as an outsider or a foreigner, but as one of your own people. Perhaps I represent the city of New-York, for I believe, as I look upon my brethren upon the platform, I am the only one who was born in the city of New-York.

This church was born one hundred years ago, just one year before my own father was born, and my father has often told me that when he was four years old, and under the care of a nurse, he was lost in the woods where the City Hall now stands; so that you see in the century of your church's life-time, how this church itself has moved three miles out of the old town where it originated. And then, when I look back fifty years, in my own life-time, I remember when Bleecker street was the last paved street in the city, north, and you are two miles outside of that town of fifty years ago; and yet you are a down-town church now. And that is the way this great city has grown, spreading not only to the north, but, as it came northward from its original little peninsula down by Wall street, spreading out east and west on its way, so that the little town of about fifteen thousand inhabitants when your church was born is now a metropolitan city of nearly one million and a half inhabitants. What a change! What a marvelous development! And when the Christian looks at that history his first thought is, with regard to this great growing city of the West, How has the kingdom of Christ prospered in it? I like very much that reference that Dr. Thomson made a few minutes ago to the witnessing of those that have gone before. I believe it from the bottom of my heart. I believe the words "Wherefore, seeing we are compassed about with so great a cloud of witnesses" mean something. The past worthies are here. They see us. I believe that our fathers and mothers of this church of New-York, of the Christian Church in the city, are witnessing what we are doing, how we are living for the Lord and His cause. The Church is one; it is a living Church, from Adam down to the last believer, always living, either in heaven or upon earth, and always united, the same family, below and above, surrounding the throne, or lifting up their prayers and their praises together to Him who is their life. Ah, it is a glorious thing to look back and feel that our pious ancestry are still with us, though we may not see them with the mortal eye. Yes, your fathers and mothers, dear friends, are here with us to-night, and they take part in our joy in commemorating the centennial anniversary of this Church of Christ. It is a glorious thought, and a very proper and appropriate thought. It makes our hearts more solemn, more courageous, more faithful, when we think of those now glorified standing by us in sympathy in all the work and conflict in which we still are placed.

Brethren, there *is* a conflict, and it is not only with the great world — that is the least conflict, after all. Of the two that I mention, the greatest conflict is with the devices of Satan within the Church of God. Read the epistles of the apostles, read the Book of Revelation, and you will find the direst enemy the truth has to contend against is the enemy within the pale of the church. Satan gets into the church and there works his evil. Now I believe the Presbyterian Church has been most free of all the denominations of Christendom from this internal power of corruption. And, under God, while I may see various causes for this, I believe one grand reason is its strong Scotch ribs. I believe that this church of yours represents that element in the Presbyterian Church in a most marked way, quite as much as when dear old Dr. Stark was your pastor, with all his strenuous earnestness. I remember him well in my boyhood. I believe that you as a church, coming right out of the Scotch parentage, are conspicuously a conservative church, conservative of God's Bible truth. And we want such churches nowadays. We want to contend against the enemy that is within us.

It has become fashionable nowadays to assimilate Christianity to human philosophy—make it all one; so that it does not make much difference whether you are a pious Buddhist, or a pious Shintoist, or a pious Greek of the old classic period, or a pious Christian; it is all the same, you have got the essential Christ in you. And that is the doctrine that is now spreading within the Church of Christ —*within the Church of Christ.* And in this great desire to break down the separating wall between Christ's gospel and the world and bring all men on a level, there are four grand heresies,—I call them heresies, with capital letters all the way through,—FOUR GRAND HERESIES that are now started in the Church of Christ. Let us look out that this doctrine does not get into the Presbyterian Church too far. It is like the camel that has got his head in. Don't let the camel get his body in.

The first error is this: Sin is not so bad a thing, after all. Sin is a misfortune, but it is not so bad. That abominable thing that God hates is not so bad, after all. That terrible lost condition of the human soul, alienated from God, is not so bad a thing, after all. It wants a little rubbing here, a little setting up there, and it will be all right; sin is not so bad a thing, after all. Well, when we have got to that pass, we don't want a Saviour. We want a helper, perhaps, a good example to encourage us in mending our ways, and to get us all right; and so Jesus Christ will be a very good example, a "monument of love"—we get some very nice terms to express what He is: He is a "monument of love"; He is an "example of beauty"; He is esthetically charming to the soul. That is what Jesus Christ is. And the whole sacrificial element of the old church means nothing at all. The cross of Christ, the blood of Christ, mean nothing at all. It is the *life* of Christ, not His death, that is now emphasized; and the death and the blood that the apostles emphasized, and that the Holy Ghost emphasized, all that is put aside, and now we are taught that it is the *life* of Christ that is so beautiful—and the life of Socrates and Confucius too. Well, so we come to two errors.

Now comes the third error: If sin is not so bad, and we don't want a Saviour, what is the use of a hell? Oh, hell was invented by Dante, or Milton, or somebody else. There comes the third error. Canon Farrar says (he is good authority just now) we are all going to be consigned to eternal hope. We read the twenty-first chapter of Matthew, third verse; after describing the wicked, it says: "These shall go away into eternal hope, and the righteous into life eternal." That is the way we read it now.

Then we have got another trouble, when we look at the New Testament. We cannot find these things. We find that sin is awful—worse than we can possibly describe or imagine. We find that the sacrifice of Jesus Christ is the expiation for sin, and His blood cleanseth from sin, and so on. We find there is a hell here.

Then we will add a fourth error: We don't believe the Bible; the Bible is not inspired any more than Milton was. That is the fourth error that comes along. Strauss began forty-five years ago to upset the New Testament. He did not succeed. He brought out the grand apologists who proved so clearly every jot and tittle of the New Testament as the word of the Lord, that Satan has now begun at the Old Testament. The cunning arch-deceiver knows that if the Old Testament goes, the New Testament goes, and Christ goes, for Christ is responsible for the Old Testament. Then they go to upsetting Moses: there never was any Moses, but somebody after Ezra's time invented the whole story commonly attributed to Moses. And if that is so, then what Christ said about Moses and the prophets is all wrong.

So Satan is working in the midst of the church to upset the Bible in that way. Now, brethren, it is your grand prerogative and your glory that you stand by the Old and the New Testament, that you stand by the truth as it has been delivered to the Saints from age to age. And this miserable new theology, which is a very old theology,—very old theology,—as old as Clement of Alexandria, as old as those first heretics who started out with Clement, as old as those heretics who tried to rope in Greek philosophy with the revelation of God—this new theology is just so old—do you stand as a strong tower against it. God bless you for it. God give you length of days and still greater strength in the mighty work. You have been a pillar of strength in this city for a hundred years. You are going to be for a hundred years to come, yea, to the millennial day; and that is the grandest wish I can have regarding you, that you will be faithful to the Word of God, that you will frame your lives according to that Word, and not according to all the philosophers and eloquent preachers, even if they be archdeacons or reverend doctors. God give you a future still more glorious than the past.

ADDRESS

BY THE

REV. JOHN HALL, D. D., LL. D.

MY DEAR CHRISTIAN FRIENDS: I was laboring under a slight mistake as to the hour when this meeting was to begin, and so I came in a little late, a circumstance for which I have to apologize, for I like to be at the beginning of every good meeting. Then I found that my brethren were under the same misapprehension, I presume, and it was suggested to me by my brother, the pastor of the church, that I should change places and make the first address, and I confess I accepted that idea with a little secret satisfaction, from the feeling that I would then have the responsibility lifted from me, and be able to listen without any reserve or anxiety about what I was to say myself, after the admirable addresses that I knew would be delivered by my brethren. They have come in, however, and taken their places, and so I come to be at the close of this very pleasant and very significant meeting.

There is one little drawback to my enjoyment in being here. I had a letter this morning from Mr. George H. Stuart, of Philadelphia, whose name is known to all of us, and who was pleased with the prospect of taking some part in these exercises; but I regret to say that the state of his health is such that his friends and medical advisers at Clifton, where he is sojourning for a time, did not approve of his coming. If he had been here, you can most of you understand, in some degree, how much heart and how much hope he would have put into the address that he would have made to you.

I have various personal reasons for being very happy in this meeting. I had the pleasure of knowing Dr. Thomson many years before I came to live in this city. I had the pleasure of having him under my roof when I was a clergyman in the capital city of my native county,

Armagh, in Ireland. Then it is rather a singular coincidence to me that in this church for the very first time I had the privilege given to me to speak a few words upon American soil. I sometimes think that I must have spoken remarkably well, for there has not been a year since when the people have not insisted upon my coming and speaking again, and it has been a very great pleasure, I am bound to say, to do it. There are other reasons, however, that lie nearer the heart, for my taking a deep interest in this congregation. I knew about it long before I saw this building; I knew about it from relatives, dear and valued kindred, who used to write to me and speak to me of the good work that was being done, and the high evangelical tone that was being maintained. I remember very well, on that first night when I came and met with the people here, being deeply impressed with the group of Elders to whom I had the pleasure of being introduced. I have rarely seen a more venerable and thoughtful-looking body of men. I think most of them, like the relatives to whom I have alluded, have finished their course, having kept the faith, and have entered into the rest that remaineth for the people of God. But their memory still lives, and I am glad to see that their children still live. You can understand how, therefore, with these pleasant associations with this church and with this people, I feel no common interest in being with you here to-night; and with all my heart I join every good wish that has been already eloquently expressed for your continued unity in the faith, your continuance in Christian living, your activity in Christian work, and your maintenance of that spirit you have attained, through which God's people are prepared on earth for enjoying the felicities of the life to come.

Allusion has been made to the large infusion of Scotch blood and character that entered into the formation, and I presume long continued in the maintenance, of this congregation. I have a very exalted idea of the many good qualities of that Scottish blood, perhaps I should say more especially after it has been carried over into the adjoining island of Ireland for five or six generations, or mingled, with wisdom and prudence, with a portion of the blood of other and kindred nations. There is no race of men upon the earth that, in view of its numbers and position, has made a more illustrious mark. There is no race that has secured a higher place in the judgment of all honest-minded and thoughtful men.

It has sometimes been alleged that there are weaknesses in the Scottish character. Well, the

Scottish people are human, and it may be expected that there will be weaknesses, but even these weaknesses can be defended if we will only take the trouble to look at them candidly. There, for example, is the statement that has gone all round the world, again and again, on very high authority, that it takes something like a surgical operation to make a Scotchman understand a joke. I think a very good reply was made to that by a Scotchman to a Southern friend who repeated that stale insinuation, and the Scotchman said quietly: "Yes, an English joke." There is no difficulty in understanding the Scottish wit, to Scottish men. In the same way it has sometimes been alleged that Scottish people are a little too persistent, the persistency amounting occasionally to obstinacy. Well, there is very much in the angle of observation at which you stand, and the standard that you have adopted in your own mind, when you are trying to judge of the character. I say that it is eminently to the credit of the Scotch people that they have such tenacity of purpose, and that, having taken hold of a thing (and they do not do it quickly), it will take a good deal to compel them to let go. Look at Scottish students. Hundreds and hundreds of them have gone to Glasgow and to Edinburgh in their poverty, entering the University, struggling with difficulty, living upon oatmeal, dressing plainly, not ashamed or afraid to work when work can be done, so as independently and upon their own resources, and without any sacrifice of self-respect, to take their places in the learned professions, in which, in so many cases, they have commanded distinguished positions.

And I am glad to say that not merely have they this tenacity of purpose, but they carry with them the religious influences under which they have been brought up. I have crossed the sea many times, and almost invariably I have found that the men who are trusted with the management of the costly machinery of our great ocean steamers are Scotchmen, whose skill and perseverance can be depended upon for the management of some of the greatest interests; and you will find the majority of them God-fearing men. I lived for some years in the western portion of my native land, where there were comparatively few Protestants, but here and there you found a Scotchman, who was a gardener, or in some position that implied superior taste and education, and you found these men everywhere lights in the place, standing up for the truth that they had been taught in the land where they received their birth and training. It is a perfectly conceivable thing that men here and there may carry a trait to that extent that it becomes open to criticism. I remember the late Dr. Stuart Robinson, a remarkably able and genial man, a Scotchman, but whose blood had come through Ireland, telling me this illustration of the very truth that I am bringing to your notice now. A Scottish man and his family moved from Scotland and went down into Kentucky; naturally the head of the family looked around to see where they would go and unite themselves for worship on the Lord's Day. They attended various churches in the neighborhood so as to try the spirits and know what was being taught there. He did not think where was the most fashionable church, or where was the church that would give him the best set-off, or anything of that sort; he wanted to know where they taught the truth, and would edify him and his family; and at last he heard a man who seemed to have just the gifts, on the whole, that would be to his comfort and instruction. But before putting in his name or doing anything to make an arrangement of a permanent sort, he respectfully requested an interview with the minister and the elders. They gave him the interview, and he told them of his history and how he had come to be there, and what his motive was in seeking this interview. "Now," he said, "I want to know this, whether are you in this congregation Burghers or Anti-burghers?" They explained, modestly, that they didn't even know the meaning of those words. "Well, no matter," he said, "I will tell you now what these words mean"; and then he explained, as only a veritable Scotchman could do, the distinction between these two sects of opinion in Scotland. And he said, "Now, brethren, suppose these issues should arise here; with which side would you array yourselves? because I want to be on the right side." I admit that that will provoke a smile on the part of almost any one; and so it should, but it is unspeakably better than that class of thinking to which Dr. Crosby has made eloquent allusion. It is unspeakably better than that carelessness, recklessness, and indifference to the things that are taught to us and to our children, provided only that they be fashionable, and that they give us a decent show of religious life as we are passing through this vale of tears.

I like the Scotch people among other things for this; that they have all along maintained such just conceptions of the real character of worship before God Almighty. I hear men talk as if the Deity were to be accounted an amateur in music. I hear men talk as if esthetics constituted the sum total of His attributes. I hear men talk as if they thought that their mere appearance in God's house on His day must necessarily be the thing which will please Him, who is a Spirit, who searches the heart, and who tries the reins of the children of men. The Scottish people have had a better idea of worship than that which we all too frequently see illustrated round about us. Of course I can understand how that conviction may be carried into regions where it will be called prejudice or bigotry. Some of you have heard the story of the good Scottish woman who was employed in the service of a very rich English lady who was in the habit of attending the cathedral, while the Scottish woman insisted on going to her own place of worship. The English woman was very anxious that her Scottish maid should once see the grandeur and beauty and irresistible charm of the cathedral service. She persuaded her one day to go and attend it, and the maid went, feeling, of course, that she was for the time doing her duty and obeying her employer. She heard the intonations and saw the procession, listened to the overtures and to the music, without saying much about it. Her employer was anxious to know what impression had been made, and she said: "Well, Janet, did you like it? What did you think of it?" "Well, ma'am, it was very nice, it was very nice,"— that was kindly to her mistress; then she began to think of what was due to her own conscience,—" But, ah, ma'am," said she, "that's an awful way to spend the Sabbath day." Yes, I like these conceptions that the Scottish people have about plain worship; and if it be one of the great purposes of the services of God's house to make people intelligent, to make them self-reliant, to make them manly, to make them courageous before their fellow-men, and meek and lowly before God, then I say these Scottish services have not failed in the purposes that Christian services contemplate. Let any one that is acquainted in any degree with Scottish history look at the influence that the people of that small and barren portion of a not very large island have exercised. Go to India—the bravest and the noblest men that have secured and held India for Great Britain have been Scottish men. I remember, when a comparatively young man, making occasional trips over to Edinburgh on church business, and in Edinburgh there lived what was called the Indian Colony. It consisted of retired officers who had served their time in India and been pensioned off. They were among the finest men that you could find in that beautiful capital. Look at the number of Scotchmen in Great Britain, and though the numbers are small, in some instances, the proportion of influence wielded by them is out of proportion to the number of Scotchmen that are there. Go over the border to Canada, in which the Scottish people have impressed their character in a great degree. You don't read the Sunday newspapers there; you don't find cars traveling on the street on Sunday. You are conscious, the moment you go into the Protestant portion of Canada, that there is an atmosphere pervading it that is only explained by the fact that the Bible has taken such hold on the conscience and thereby molded to such a great extent the habits of the people.

I like the system that the Scottish people fell upon through the study of God's word for managing the affairs of the church, and promoting great spiritual interest, and I would like to see you Protestants—I do not speak for myself; I speak for one of the great historians of England, who was by no means a particularly religious or spiritual man, who says, in effect, that the ways of dealing with any religious question in Scotland are very remarkable; they have their General Assembly, and they have their Synod, and they have their Presbytery, and they have their Kirk-session, and they have their Congregation; and when any great question arises, it is discussed in the Assembly, and it is discussed in the Synod, and it is discussed in the Presbytery, and it is discussed in the Kirk-session, and it is discussed all over the parish. "And what is the consequence?" he said. "Why, these Scottish people know with astonishing intelligence the merits of every great question of this kind." And he adds (and this is the point that I would emphasize): "Hence the remarkable distinction between England and Scotland." England has an established church, with great wealth, with the universities and kindred institutions under its control; with prestige, with power, with authority, with everything that might make up the church of the masses of the people. But what is the consequence? What is the effect? Why, more than one-half of the population of England have gone out of that established church. And where have they gone? Have they gone to get a purer Episcopal church? A better hierarchy? Nothing of the kind. Almost without exception they have gone as far away as they could from everything that was distinctive of the national church,—away from the bishops, away from the hierarchy, away from the ritual, away from everything except what they accounted spiritual freedom. Go into Scotland, on the other hand. Scotland, to-day, has dissenting bodies. There have been United Presbyterians, Associate Presbyterians, Reformed Presbyterians, Free-church Presbyterians; but in every case where these people have left the establishment in Scotland, it has been, not to get as far away from Presbyterianism as they could, but to get, as they believed, a better

Presbyterianism, free from the faults and errors and mistakes into which they believed the mother church, for the time, had been led. And as to the tenacity of belief, we know, as a matter of fact, that the people of consequence, the gentry and land-owners, almost to a man, have associated themselves with the church that is in power in England, and they have many times been a little unscrupulous in the effort to push the interests of their church; and with what results? About two hundred congregations of that order is the whole amount of what they have been enabled to secure in Scotland, and some of these congregations are extremely small.

Now on these grounds I say I cannot but have a strong preference for Scottish thought and Scottish ways, and for the distinctive features of the Scottish character, and I do hope that these features will never be totally obliterated in this Christian congregation. You have round about you the varied tints of autumnal leaves, beautiful in decay. They are not to represent this congregation. If they do represent anything, it will be the hoary heads that I see in numbers scattered over this flock. But if you want something here that is to represent this congregation, let it be these evergreens on the right hand and on the left, that through all seasons keep their color, that through all seasons have the look of vigor and prosperity about them.

Allusion was made in a very genial way (Dr. Ormiston never does anything that is not in a genial way) to the greater antiquity of the brethren of the Reformed Church, of which he is a brilliant and honored, as well as useful, pastor; and he even suggested that if we of the General Assembly should want to make a change again, or, at least, if this congregation should want to make a change again, there will be a pleasant home within the borders of our brethren of the Reformed Church. It is like his greatness of heart; it is like his magnanimity. But there is another way of looking at it. Call that church the mother church, if you like, and this, and even the whole general assembly to which it belongs, a daughter; call it so, if you please. I have known many happy cases where the dear, venerable, aged mother, become a grandmother, has gone into the dwelling of the daughter and been cared for with as much sweetness and love as ever she had in her own home. And if anything like this should ever transpire here, it will be a common joy and gladness to all of us.

The truth is (and this is the last word that I want to say, because it is not proper to detain you too long), we are reformed Christians: We are a Reformed Church, thank God, and I hope we shall stand fast by the reformation. My brother Kerr and I are United Presbyterians. There used to be an old school and a new school; but we are United Presbyterians, and I should be delighted if the so-called United Presbyterians that are in this city and round about us would take us into their ranks, and the General Assembly include these different bodies of practically the same church. It would be a great deal better for them to come and join with us, than to be divided into so many branches. I remember many years ago meeting a most brilliant United Presbyterian minister, who came over to visit us in Dublin, and in the course of a genial speech that he made there, in which we were alternatingly laughing and weeping, he made this statement, which I never forgot. He said: "For the sake of brevity, the people call us United Presbyterians, ' U. P's,' and we must take care never to divide up again, for if we did, they would be sure to call us 'split peas' ever after."

And there is another branch, the Covenanters. Brethren, I am a Covenanter. I adhere in the main to the distinctive principle of the so-called Covenanters of the ancient days. I love their memory; I revere their spirit. I am proud of having hereditary union with them. I am glad to think that members of my own household are among their ranks to-day. And I shall be glad when all this general assembly, when the General Assembly of the Southern Church, Dutch Reformed, United Presbyterians, and Covenanters, joined in one, shall be found bearing testimony heartily and unitedly to that great evangelical truth which is the glory of the church, which it is our business to maintain, and by the proclamation of which issues a blessing continually to the wide world.

Tuesday, October 27, 1885.—7.30 P. M.

Addresses by the

Rev. Henry M. Field, D. D.

Rev. R. R. Booth, D. D.

Rev. W. M. Taylor, D. D., LL. D.

The Pastor presided, and was assisted by the Revs. S. B. Rossiter and T. W. Chambers, D. D., LL. D.

ADDRESS

BY THE

REV. HENRY M. FIELD, D. D.

MY DEAR BRETHREN: When you listen to such a ringing voice as that of your pastor, you need few words from others. But certainly it is a privilege to me, and a privilege to all these brethren who are here to-night, to come in and look in your faces, and join in your hymns, and listen to the prayers that are offered; to give united thanks to Almighty God that He has preserved this church for a hundred years. A hundred years! a century! That is a long stretch in the life of man, or in the life of generations. We are accustomed to reckon thirty years as the life of a generation, since that on the average is about the active period of a man's life; and hence he who keeps watch of the current of human activity, who keeps his eye on the column as it is marching on, will, in the course of thirty years, see one generation of workers pass off the stage, and another come up upon it. And so we may reckon that in the last hundred years three generations have passed off the stage; those that were children, yea, those that were not born a hundred years ago, have come into life, have been children, have been young men and women, have performed the duties of manhood and womanhood, have grown to old age and passed away, to be succeeded by others; while this Church of Christ has remained the same. Here the altar has stood, here the fire has burned, from generation to generation; and here we hope in God the fire is to burn for a hundred years to come.

We rejoice, my dear brethren, in all the memories of the past, the memories of the living and the dead. You recall, as you sit here in these seats, those honored fathers and mothers, who "have all died in faith, and have inherited the promises." You remember the tender and sacred beauty of those characters which were patterns to their children; you mark them, as they pass through all the stages of life till its close, preserving the same serenity and sweetness and peace unto the end. When they passed away, they left to you, their survivors, the rich inheritance of their example.

How much there is in the review of a hundred years to encourage our faith in God, our faith in that overruling providence which controls all the affairs of men, of churches, and of nations! How we see the hand of God in the history of our country! A hundred years ago this nation was just emerging from the long eight-years' war which ended in independence. The country was poor, thinly settled, weak, with everything yet to be done; and yet how wonderful has been its career! Within a hundred years it has passed through periods of adversity, through financial distresses, through wars with foreign nations, and, worse than all, through the greatest civil war of modern times; but all these trials have come and gone, and still the nation lives. And so may we say, with more emphasis still, the Church lives, in spite of all attacks upon her; and so the Church will live in the hundred years to come.

I am not going to say much, because here behind me sits my brother, Dr. Booth, who has just returned from the East, who has seen what is going on there in that old world, which is becoming the new world. We are accustomed to say, in our vanity: "Westward the star of empire takes its way." So it does, but in time the star of empire may go down in the West, and rise again in the East. He who looks toward the dawn will see the curtain rise on great events, and that before many years. Such events are already transpiring. To-day the attention of the whole world is attracted to Turkey, that borderland between Europe and Asia, where, even at this very moment, there are wars and rumors of wars, the signs of great changes both in the political and the religious world. Dr. Booth has just passed through that country, and can describe it with all the vividness of a recent witness. Only yesterday I was at a breakfast given to Archdeacon Farrar, to which were invited representatives of the press, and beside me sat the editor of the *Evening Post*, who, twenty years and more ago, was the correspondent of the *London News* in the Crimean war; and he said to me as we talked of the East, "One day that I was at Belgrade, I saw a courier ride into that city, who had come all the way from Constantinople, riding nine days and nights; for the rule was that he should never dismount from his horse, except to eat— not to sleep; for he was to sleep on horseback. When horses were to be changed, he did not dismount, but was lifted from one horse to another, so that his feet should not touch the ground till he had passed over that immense distance from Constantinople to Belgrade!" Nine days and nights! and now soon the iron horse will carry all the couriers and all the travelers over that immense distance within twenty-four hours! So the ends of the world are coming together.

And there are great changes going on in the religious world. One of the most gratifying things to the traveler in the East is to see what has been done by missionaries, and by American missionaries; how their little churches and their schools dot all European and Asiatic Turkey, and how they have built great colleges on the Bosphorus, and at Beirut, overlooking the Mediterranean, and at Aintab and Kharpoot, in the interior of Asiatic Turkey.

But I must not stop to speak of this. The hand of God is in all this pressing, moving tide. The world is going on; the Church is making progress; and it is a blessed thing for us all to live in this time and to have some part, however humble, in this great work that is to be done for the world and for our divine Lord and Master.

A hundred years to come! Long before that period shall arrive, all of us will have passed away; the youngest child that is here will be numbered with the dead; but the Church will live. It will live from generation to generation, for centuries and millenniums, and the cause of Christ will spread over America, over Africa, over Asia, till the whole world shall be filled with the knowledge of God, as the waters cover the sea.

My brethren, I congratulate you with all my heart on this anniversary; I rejoice with you, and join in your thanksgivings to God for all that He has done in you and by you in this city. And I pray for God's blessing upon you, not only in the happy services of this week, but in all the future of your lives, in your homes, and in this church where you commune and labor together; I pray that as you increase in years you may increase in all wisdom and virtue, abounding in every good work; and thus doing, as individuals and as a church, more and more for the honor of your Lord and for the salvation of the world.

ADDRESS

BY THE

REV. R. R. BOOTH, D. D.

DEAR FRIENDS: I feel like Joseph's brethren, in respect to penitence, as I stand here to-night. They said, when they were in trying circumstances in the matter of Joseph, that they remembered their misdeeds that day; and I am in a measure afflicted and humiliated as I stand before you, to realize that really this is the first time that I have ever stood in this pulpit, or looked into the face of this noble congregation. I don't know how it has come to pass, certainly not in the years gone by for the lack of cordial invitations,—several, at least, from your pastor,—but so it was. And I feel especially grateful and gratified for the welcome given to me in such kind words, as I now stand in this beautiful edifice, and behold so many evidences of the prosperity of the church, aside from this centennial anniversary. This is indeed, I believe, a unique occasion in the history of the Presbyterian Churches in our city. Our brother, Dr. Chambers, tells me, with that sense of self-possession which becomes a son of the Reformed Church, that they have celebrated their quarter-millennial — their two hundred and fiftieth anniversary. But we Presbyterians have never aspired to any such longevity as that; at least, we are very far from having attained it. I do not remember that the First Presbyterian Church, which is the mother of us all, celebrated the event when it reached its centennial year. What has become of the Second and the Third Churches, I don't know; it has been a matter of inquiry among us here upon the platform. The surmise is, that the Second Church is that which is known as the "Brick Church," and the Third is the Scotch Church in Fourteenth street. Whether they have observed a centenary, I don't know. But I think you have done well on this occasion in bringing to remembrance the years gone by: "I have thought of Thy loving-kindness, O God," said the psalmist, "in the midst of Thy Temple." And I especially realize the gladness and the interest of this occasion, in looking upon two of the forms that are present with us to-night, who have, doubtless, been present on former occasions during the week—our honored friend, Dr. Thomson, who was here when I came into this neighborhood many, many years ago, and who has not only favored his own former congregation, but has shed a benignant light upon all his ministerial brethren of New-York, in coming across the sea from "old Scotland" to see us all again. May he return in health and in prosperity, and may his days be long and happy in the dear old motherland which every Presbyterian loves. And we are happy, also, in the presence of our beloved brother, Dr. Spaulding, whose face is always radiant with a benediction for those who love the Kingdom of God, and whose songs, as you have sung them here, make one wonder at the fertility and at the readiness with which his thought flows into these sacred verses.

Brethren, it is a good thing to be a Presbyterian. I don't know that it is the best thing; the best of all is to be a Christian; but to be a Presbyterian intelligently, with clear convictions, is, I think, the best form of being a Christian that this world in its present state knows of.

Allusion has been made to the fact that I have been moving to and fro upon the earth, and looking at different peoples and at different institutions in many lands. I hope I have been learning from my experience in these past two and a half years, as I had learned, somewhat before, to exercise a spirit of charity toward those who differed from me. The Christian world is full of many differing churches. When we look at our own church and our own system, we should value ourselves overmuch, if we should imagine that we were the whole or that we were a very large part of the whole; and one must in all Christian charity realize in the presence of those churches of the East, and in those churches of southern Europe, where there is such devotion, such self-sacrifice, such earnest religious zeal according to their light, that we should do ourselves and our Master wrong if we should assume to be the only church. And yet that we are a church of which we need not be ashamed is certainly true. Some four or five weeks ago, I had the opportunity of being present in the city of Edinburgh and joining in the worship of some of the congregations, and in visiting again, not for the second or the third time, some of those historic spots. I don't know that I have felt more proud of our Presbyterian record than when I stood in Greyfriar's Church-yard and looked upon the graves of the martyred Scotch ministers and noblemen who, to the number of one hundred and fifty, lie buried in an inconspicuous corner, the ground that holds their honored remains marked only by a monument of recent erection, telling the story of their life and of their death, and how they perished in the strife for the Church of God, and for his covenant, under the blue Presbyterian flag. I feel that in all our history as a church we have much to rejoice over and to be proud of, and especially in our connection with the dear Scottish brethren. My heart has always warmed toward the Scottish men wherever I have found them. It was my privilege during this winter to act as a kind of minister at intervals to a section of the Scottish Presbyterian nation that was assembled for warlike purposes in the city of Cairo, assisting, by a curious coincidence, as it has been suggested to me by Dr. Thomson, one of the boys from his Scottish parish, Rev. Mr. Robertson, who is the chaplain of the "Black Watch," or 42d Highlanders. And there they gathered, in our chapel services in Cairo, Sabbath after Sabbath, and even during the week, those stalwart Scottish soldiers, clad in the Highland costume; and one felt in looking at their faces that any cause that was intrusted to their hands was safe as far as human courage could make it so, and all the safer because they were so largely men of God.

One's mind during the past winter in that part of the world to which I have alluded has been very much turned to Scottish interests, not only by the regiments, but also by the number of noble men who have played their part, and many of whom have fallen a sacrifice in that ill-fated expedition in the Soudan. How many of them I saw during the early months of this year passing southward toward the Soudan or the Red Sea—noble men, beginning with Gordon, the leader, and the hero of Khartoum. I was sitting one evening in the house of an English officer in the Khedive's service, when this last letter of General Gordon was placed in my hands. I don't know that it has ever been made public—the last lines that fell from his pen:

"MY DEAR WATSON: The game is up, and I write to make my adieus to yourself and to your wife and to some other friends. This would not have happened, if it does happen, if our people had taken pains to let me know of their plans, and had been a little earlier. As it now seems, the catastrophe cannot be delayed longer than ten or twelve days. But this is spilt milk. Good-bye."

This is the last word that came to us from that Scottish Presbyterian, Gordon, who has been worthy of his clan and worthy of his record. But now our minds turn back to a hundred years ago, when this church was founded on its narrow foundations. How great the change since then! George the Third was on the throne of England. Napoleon Bonaparte, a young lieutenant in Paris, was playing chess on the table that still stands, with the inscription recording the fact, in the Café de la Régime. All Europe was in the night of the middle ages. Practically, the Holy Inquisition was in full sway in Spain and in Rome, and the ambassadors of the European courts, as they presented themselves at the Sublime Porte, went humbly upon their knees and kissed the dirt, as became envoys from an almost unknown world. How changed these things are at the present day! Allusion has been made to the Turkish Empire, and to American enterprise in connection with it. It is an illustration, and therefore I speak of it, of what is accomplished sometimes by the influence of a single church, moving through a variety of avenues, working out results which at the time of their inception are often hard to understand or to anticipate. On the banks of the Bosphorus there stands an institution that bears the name of Robert College, the name of a not now living, but once honored merchant of this city, who was a member of the Session in the Brainerd Church, a church that was founded long after this church took its rise. Traveling in the East for purposes of recreation, his mind was struck with the need of education, as well as missionary effort and instruction, in the Turkish Empire. The outcome of his interest was the founding of Robert College, which it was intended should furnish missionaries and ministers from the native population. Robert College was founded some twenty years ago, and among the first students who came to it was a company whose presence and whose interest in the institution was entirely unexpected,—a company of Bulgarian youth, whose language at that time was strange to the missionaries, and whose appearance was most uncouth, betokening social degradation and the lack of cultivated manners. It so turned out, in the providence of God, that Robert College, which was intended especially for the education of Greek and Turkish youth, became the center of a Bulgarian educational system, which in the course of time sent back hundreds and hundreds of Bulgarian young men into that province, who gradually entered into prominent places, first as school-masters, then as teachers, and then, by their administrative skill, as prefects and sub-prefects in the State under the Turkish establishment. These men were educated in Protestant evangelical ideas, and from the American social and political point of view. Now the presence of these men in Bulgaria gradually caused the uplifting of the people to a higher standard of education and to a larger estimate of that which was necessary for the liberty and well-being of the people. As the result of this restlessness came the terrible massacres of which you all have heard. Out of these massacres came the intervention of Russia, and the Turko-Russian war, the issue of which was the practical sundering of the Turkish Empire, the establishment of the kingdom of Servia and the kingdom of Roumania, and the virtual enfranchisement of Bulgaria, which has now been consummated by the addition of the southern section, the province of Roumelia, which the treaty of Berlin took away. Nothing is more certain, in the line of direct result following cause, than that the establishment of Robert College and the gifts of Christopher Robert, a noble member of a Presbyterian Session in this city, led to the breaking up, so far as it has been accomplished, of the Turkish Empire, and the beginning of a new day throughout the East. It is worth while for a minister to have a well-trained Session, and to give it scope, and in our Presbyterian system a faithful elder, blessed with means and heart, may be expected to devise great things for the Kingdom of God.

I give you another illustration. As one travels farther East, he comes to that most beautiful of Oriental cities for situation, the city of Beirut, a city of a hundred thousand people, lying on the slopes of Lebanon, and largely civilized, according to our American conception of civilization; and there, on one of the heights that overlook the sea, stands a college, not a whit inferior to Robert College in its equipment, in the staff of instructors, and in all those influences that work upon a nation's life. That college, too, was founded by another member of the Session of that same Brainerd Church, in association with other men. And so, from that single point of view, from the developed life of the single church of which I speak, there have arisen two institutions that under God are doing more to change the face of that dark Eastern world than all the diplomacy of Europe put together. I saw a letter the other day from Dr. Washburne, of Robert College, describing a visit which he was making, in a quiet way, into Bulgaria just before the recent outbreak, when the people thronged about him and followed him from town to town, and at last took the horses from his carriage and drew him in triumph through the streets; so heartily did they recognize what they owed to that man, and to the institution which he represented, out of which had come their liberties and their hopes.

Brethren, the greatest thing in this world, as one may look upon it with a sympathetic Christian eye, is the Church of Christ, in its onward, its aggressive movement to overcome the world for the Redeemer. The church that lives a hundred years, and holds its own, and does a work that reaches far away beyond its own circumference, has great cause to thank God, and to take courage for the hundred years to come. We have been living in the grandest century of the six thousand years or more of our world's history; and in the life of those who have made the successive generations of this church, all the great institutions that are changing the face of society and uplifting the world have been born. Less than a hundred years ago, Carey and his associates went to India — Dr. Taylor asks me not to steal his thunder; but he is a busy man, and I am an idle man, and I must take what comes to me just as it occurs. Less than a hundred years ago, Carey and his associates went to India, and Sidney Smith (that witty English prelate) said that "they were a handful of maniacs going out to convert a hundred millions of men." It is true they have not all been converted, but the civilization that has reached beyond these missionary efforts is a product of which the thoughtful Christian man must constantly take cognizance. Less than a hundred years ago, the young men of Williams College gathered around the haystack under which they found shelter in a thunder-storm, and planned the great American missionary enterprise. Less than a hundred years ago, Dr. Taylor and brethren, of Scotland, the burghers of Inverness, coming together for a friendly talk, said one to another, that they had heard of a town named Dingwell, away up in the mud and among the rocks, fifteen miles to the north of them, and sent out a deputation to search it out. Less than a hundred years ago, the world was large because communication was so difficult and long; now the world is small; and, dear brethren and friends, the omnipresent person in the world is Jesus Christ, our King, moving on in the mighty path of His salvation. All the advantages of our time are associated in some way with the uplifting and civilizing and sanctifying work of His dear church; and those whose hearts are united unto Him and to His blessed work, while they cannot trace the diverging and extending lines of the influence that they put forth, may be sure that He who reigns above will use these influences, if they are put forth in loyalty to Him, so that the little one shall become a thousand, and the small one as a strong nation.

Dear friends, I had many things to say, but Dr. Taylor's interruption shows me how eager he is to get to his feet and speak. On occasions like this he is irrepressible, and I shall not long restrain him.

The pastor asks me to speak of a single incident, or of a single phase that presents itself to one who travels in the northern part of Italy. God's hidden ones are spoken of in the Bible. Some of us discovered a year or two ago, just where the northern part of Italy meets the southern part of Switzerland, a half a dozen churches that had been buried for two hundred and fifty years in isolation because there were no roads, no communication, no travel. They were churches of the Reformation, that had been formed in the Presbyterian order, and they had lived in loneliness, and maintained their faith and order until they were excavated by the visitation of some who came on the roads while civil-engineering, and they have begun to live a new life, and are doing good things in missionary effort all over that region. And so, if I had time, I might speak to you of that great realm of Italy, next to Great Britain and our own, the most progressive land, I think, on earth, where the old Waldensian Church, one of the sister churches of the Reformation, is girding itself anew with power and reaching far and wide with wondrous evangelical efforts. But I must tell you of a single thing, in the way of a mere incident, as indicating what a sympathetic look or word sometimes accomplishes. I happened, a few months ago, to be passing through Verona, a city lying between Valencia and Milan, on the Sabbath day, and it occurred to me to visit the Waldensian Church, to attend the church and speak with the people. The pastor, at the close of the service, said to me, when I told him I was a Presbyterian minister from New-York, and my wife was a Presbyterian Church member: "I have heard of such persons; I have heard of Presbyterian ministers and members; but I never saw one in my life before." And they were passing through Verona by hundreds and almost by thousands every year. And he, in the sense of contact with a living embodiment of something Presbyterian from the other side, seemed to take upon himself a new stature, and his face shone with a new joy, and so, brethren, in a thousand ways, a sympathetic word is a word that tells for God.

The continuance of the church on earth in itself is a perpetual shining of a light that spreads out into the darkness. May your light long continue to shine, not as in the past, but brighter and brighter, to the perfect day; and may unnumbered benedictions rest upon you, and upon your beloved pastor, always.

Address

BY THE

Rev. W. M. Taylor, D. D., LL. D.

I AM always glad to be neighborly, for I have good neighbors about me, and "a man that hath friends must show himself friendly."

This church has been a good neighbor to me. In the days of my friend, the predecessor of your beloved pastor, when there was no roof over our heads on the opposite corner, you opened your door for us, and we had evening service here, for, I think, two or three months. That was a neighborly act that I have never forgotten and never can forget. And I feel that anything that I can do for this church and for its pastor is little in comparison to that great favor which was rendered by the church here to us in our circumstances of need. It has been my good fortune to live on terms of brotherhood and love with all my brethren here. I think never a man, coming as I did among entire strangers, received such a royal welcome from his brethren in the ministry as I did. And even if some of them were a little inclined to be offish, they by and by turned out to be my most affectionate friends. So that I should be one of the most ungrateful of men if I did not willingly put myself about, if that were needed, to show my brotherhood to those who took me by the hand when I was an utter stranger in this city and this land, and came to a congregation, only one or two members of which had ever seen me in the flesh until I stood in their pulpit. I shudder sometimes when I think what I did then. As I said to a brother of mine to-day, nothing but the firmest persuasion, that in taking the step which I then took I was following the clearest command of my Master, would have sustained me in the sacrifices which I made and the experiences through which I passed. When I was half-way across the Atlantic, it dawned upon me that I had burned the boats behind me, and that I was going to a place I did not know. Who was to meet me on the wharf,

I could not tell. I never had seen them; and if it had not been for one little sentence of the book of Genesis, that came to me, as I have no doubt now, by the suggestion of God's Spirit, I do not know what I should have done. That sentence was: "I being in the way, the Lord led me." That has held me all these years. That keeps me yet; and the welcome which I got, not only from my own people, but from the brethren of the city generally, makes me think that I should be the most ungrateful of men, if I did not on all occasions, whenever it is possible, hold myself at their disposal to render them whatever service they may require. Some people say that it is easier to weep with them that weep than to rejoice with them that rejoice. I question whether that is true in my case. I am sure that my heart to-night is full of joy and gratitude for you, when in the retrospect of a hundred years you have come here to raise your Ebenezer as a Christian church, and to say: "Hitherto the Lord hath helped us."

Now in settling what I should speak about to-night, I thought it would be well just to look at two or three things in which we have made extraordinary progress in the Christian church during the last hundred years. One of these was that to which my brother, Dr. Booth, was referring when I rather improperly interrupted him. I mean activity in the cause of foreign missions. Some ninety years ago, I think in the year 1796, there was a famous debate on missions in the General Assembly of the Church of Scotland. Perhaps some of you may be familiar with the incidents and individuals of that discussion, as they have been described by the master hand of Hugh Miller, in the sketch which has been preserved in one of the volumes of his collected works. It is rather singular reading in these days. Two overtures came up—I need not explain to a Presbyterian Church what an overture is—from different Synods, one asking the Assembly in general terms to give its approval of the work of foreign missions, and the other asking the Assembly to do something specific in entering upon a foreign mission of its own. These overtures were brought before the Assembly in due form, and the adoption of one of them was moved by a man whose name comes into prominence in Robert Burns's poems, not entirely to his credit, for in after-life he did not shine very brightly. He was there in the Assembly as an elder; his name was Robert Heron. The motion was seconded by the Reverend Dr. John Erskine, who was prevented, however, at that time from making his speech by some form of the House; and the rejection of the overture was moved by no less a person than Dr. George Hill, the Professor of Divinity in St. Andrew's, and the Principal of St. Andrew's University, whose "Lectures on Theology" was one of the text-books of Chalmers at a later day in his class. Even such a man as Hill, who was the leader of the Moderate party of the house at that time, moved the rejection of the overture, and Hamilton of Gladsmuir seconded its rejection. After they had said some very strong things about the proposals,—had, in fact, called them the schemes of hare-brained enthusiasts, and the most absurd things that had ever been put upon the table of the house,—Erskine rose. There was a Bible on the desk in front of the Moderator, as there always is at a meeting of the General Assembly in Scotland, and he said, "Moderator, rax me that Bible"; and, with the Bible open, he began to expound to them the duty of entering on the missionary enterprise. But such was the weight of prejudice and ignorance in that Assembly, that—it is hardly possible to believe it now—the overtures were rejected by a most overwhelming majority. And that was not quite a hundred years ago.

As I have just spoken of John Erskine, let me say that he was the colleague of Robertson the historian, who was himself a very strong Moderate. The colleague, however, was a man of a different type, and you will find a most admirable description of him given by Walter Scott in his novel of "Guy Mannering." But more to the present purpose, and more interesting to us on this side of the Atlantic now, is the fact that this John Erskine was the first Scotchman who lifted up his voice in indignant protest against the conduct of the British government toward these American colonies; and his pamphlet, entitled "Ought we to go to War with our American Brethren?" is a production of very great power, filled, too, with scathing indignation, and not without its interest even in the present day. He had good reason to love these American colonies, for he was a close friend and constant correspondent of Jonathan Edwards, of New England; and in the memoir of that great man you will find that some of the best letters which it contains are those which he wrote to and those which he received from John Erskine. Now, only think, that was but about ninety years ago. Since then, what has Scotland done in the great missionary cause? I recall, for example, the names of Morrison and Legge, who went out to China in connection with the London Missionary Society; those of Moffate and Livingstone, who went to Africa in connection with the same society, and that of Duff, who went out some thirty or forty years after from the very Church of Scotland in the Assembly of which that great debate was held. And as I repeat those names, and bring up before you all that is associated with them, you will understand what immense progress we have made in this matter of Christian missions during these hundred years. As Dr. Booth has said, it is only seventy-five years since the American Board was formed,— we were holding its seventy-fifth anniversary just a few days ago in Boston,— and to-day its missionaries are all over the world. There are besides, English and Scottish missionaries in Japan, China, India, South Africa, Central Africa, Western Africa, in the West India Islands, all along down the eastern coast of South America, and up the western coast. Now, that is something to be thankful for, proving, as it does, that we are living in one of the greatest and most progressive of the centuries that the world has seen since the days of the apostles.

But not only in connection with foreign missions have we seen such wonderful advance. Equal progress is conspicuous in the activity of the churches at home. In the memorable debate to which I have referred, there was one brother — I am ashamed to say his name was Dr. William Taylor, of Glasgow — who stood up and said, "We cannot entertain this proposition, because there are heathen enough at home to work for, and it will be time enough for us to go abroad when we have evangelized those at our own doors." Well, we have heard that a great many times since then, but if that were a valid excuse for neglecting foreign missions, then surely, before the foreign missionary enterprise was entered upon, we might expect to find a great deal of activity at home; and that the churches were earnestly at work for the elevation and evangelization of those around them. But was that so? Go back a hundred years: Were there any Sunday-schools then? Perhaps you might have found a few, for the centenary of the Sunday-school was observed in London and on this side of the water in 1880, but they were few and far between. Would you have found any city missions? Not one. City missions were the creation of the early part of this century, and the name of David Naismith comes into prominence in connection with them; not the Naismith that is famous for the invention of the steam-hammer, but he who went down into the depths of London slums and brought up thence precious souls, that he might set them as jewels in the coronet of the Redeemer. And from London the city mission enterprise spread over all the large cities and towns of England and Scotland, and we have had the benefit of it here also. Were there any Scripture-readers in those days? No, none at all. Were there district visitors? None. Was there any tract distribution? Not at all. All these enterprises of Christian benevolence and activity which we now see so earnestly at work, and to which we of the present generation have been accustomed almost from our earliest days, are themselves the fruits of the revived Christianity of the churches during the last hundred years. That is a great thing to be thankful for, and it becomes us to see that we, on whom the latter part of the century has fallen, shall not allow these works to fail. We ought to pledge ourselves by the memory of our fathers to carry forward to yet more glorious triumphs the enterprises of Christian aggressiveness both at home and abroad, with which so many of them were so conspicuously identified.

Then, again, this century has seen wonderful progress in the matter of Christian brotherhood and love. I think the previous century was perhaps, at least among Presbyterians,— I suppose I may speak about that, because I am two-thirds of a Presbyterian at least, perhaps more,— I think the last century among Presbyterians may be called a century of divisions. There was a tendency to magnify points into principles, and if these points were not all conceded, an immediate division was the result. When my friend Dr. Booth was speaking about the Burghers of Inverness, I did not know whether he meant simply the citizens of Inverness or another kind of Burghers altogether. I wonder how many of this congregation know about Burghers and Anti-burghers. There were five towns in Scotland that had connected with them an oath which had to be taken by every burgess. Every one who had conferred upon him the freedom of the town, as it was called, had to take an oath which bound him to do nothing that was contrary to the interests of the Protestant religion as by law established in the land. Well, you would not think that there was much about that to discuss; but controversy over it got into the Secession Church in the early years of its history, I suppose before it completed the first twenty years of its history, and although there were very few of the members of the Secession Church in these five towns, yet the contest waxed hot and heavy, whether it was proper for one who was a member of the Secession Church to take that oath. Some said it was warrantable enough to take it. They said that it meant simply that they were not to favor Roman Catholicism. Others said it was wrong to take it, because it meant that they were not to do anything against the Scotch Established Church, from which they had seceded. And so the controversy waxed grievous, until at length there was a division of the denomination over it into two, and those of them who thought there was no harm in taking the burgess oath were called Burghers, and those who thought it was wrong to take the burgess oath were called Anti-burghers; and the conflict was very, very bitter between them. Members of the same families, arrayed on different sides of the question, would be so bitter that they would not speak to each other on the subject. My grandfather was on the one side and my grandmother on the other. And when the minister of my grandmother, who was on the Burgher side, came to the house when my grandfather was ill, the sick man was so strong and rigid, so conscientious in his adherence to what he thought was principle, that he would not consent to see him, even although he believed him to be a Christian man. And the children learned from the parents the same kind of feeling. A very good story used to be told in illustration of that. One Sacramental Sunday evening, when the preaching was in the open air, the boys who were on the outskirts of the crowd were somewhat noisy, and the minister of the church (it was a Relief Church), whose place was being occupied by a brother, thought he would go round and restore quiet. As he approached the disturbers of the peace, the boys took to their heels, but one poor fellow fell, and as the minister caught hold of him, the other mischievous fellows, standing at a safe distance, cried out: "Lick him weel, sir; his fayther's an Anti-burgher." That story well illustrates the temper of the time, and will help you to understand what I mean when I say that Presbyterians a hundred years ago were a great deal more given to breaking up into fragments over little points than they were to coming together. But now for the last sixty-five years or so the tide has turned, and the wave is flowing in the direction of brotherhood and love and union. Those two fractions, as we may call them, of the Secession Church came together in the year 1820, and the union came about because they had got to praying together, first, in little fellowship prayer-meetings. Then, in the year 1847, the Relief Church went in and formed with them what is now in Scotland the United Presbyterian Church. And the same thing has been going on elsewhere. We have had a rising tide of Christian union during all these years, and a very blessed thing it is; and very much of it has been the result of the activity of Christian churches of all denominations in foreign missions and in home effort. Almost all the Presbyterian Churches and the Congregational Board have missionaries now in India; many of them, or most of them, have missionaries in Japan and China and elsewhere. Those brethren out there in the front, among the heathen, could not help coming close together. It is a very close communion out there, but it is not a close communion that excludes; it is a close communion that embraces, because the heathen are round about them; and coming thus into close communion and close coöperation with each other, they learned thereby the good that is in each other. If you go to Europe, and a person who lives in the same street with you, to whom you have never spoken before, and who has never spoken to you before, should see you walking in the streets of London, I will venture to say that he would make straight for you, and say, "How do you do? What are you doing here?" because distance from home and isolation has led you to appreciate each other. I remember once going into the Langham Hotel in London, when a man came up to me and said, "Dr. Taylor, how do you do? I am glad to see you. I have seen your wife since you did." "Yes, but I do not know you." "Why," said he, "I live in your street. I have never spoken to you before, but I could not well let you go past here." Well, it was just similar with our missionaries of different denominations in the high places of foreign heathenism. There they were thrown together and learned to love each other, and the influence of that came home and the brethren here began to look into each other's faces and into each other's hearts, and the Evangelical Alliance was the result. The same thing is true in regard to our coöperation at home. Brethren of all denominations sit together on the committees of the Tract Society, and the Bible Society, and the City Mission Society, and they cannot meet there without seeing the good that is in each other; and thus there has been during these last eighty years a very great increase in the spirit of Christian union. We may not have gone into each other's churches and said, this is just as good as my own; but we have conversed with each other over the partition walls, and the partition walls are not nearly so high now as they were years ago. By and by, perhaps, they may be lower still; but, at any rate, it is a great thing to say that the churches, as a whole, are growing in the spirit which the Redeemer prayed for when He said: "That they all may be one, as Thou, Father, art in me, and I in Thee; that they all may be one in us."

And then (this is the last thing that I will refer to) we have come to see more clearly, during these hundred years, the difference between essentials and non-essentials in religious matters. That is just stating in another way what I have already said, but it is important enough to be emphasized. Now I don't see it, but I know it is up there [pointing to the organ]. A hundred years ago that would not have been there, and much less than a hundred years ago the attempt to put it there would have been met by a storm of opposition. But we have now come more than before to regard it as not a matter of great moment. We have come to see that the one great scriptural rubric in regard to praise is: "God is a spirit, and they that worship Him must worship Him in spirit and in truth." Give us these two things, and wherever you have these, organ or no organ, the worship is acceptable to God. Then there is another point: you have here what I am delighted to see, these hymns. Well, I am old enough to remember when there was only one Presbyterian denomination in Scotland, and that the Relief Church, that sang hymns. I remember the introduction of the hymn-book into the United Presbyterian Church of Scotland. It is only within the last few years that hymns have been introduced into the Established Church of Scotland. The Congregational Churches, I believe, from the very beginning of their history in Scotland, under the Haldanes, sang hymns; but the Presbyterian Churches, with the exception of the Relief Church, had no hymns, save the paraphrases. Now we have got to see that just as we pray in uninspired language, so we may sing uninspired hymns. And yet, let me say this: although it is a great thing to have these hymns, and although there are things in the New Testament which I want to sing about, and for which I cannot always find an appropriate psalm (for instance, the resurrection of the Lord Jesus Christ, and all that I owe to that—except the Sixteenth Psalm, I think there is not any one that refers to that, and I want to sing about that very often), still, although that is the case, it is a great regret to me that in my church hymn-book we have few metrical psalms. And I am delighted to know that in the front part of your hymn-book here you have selections from the old psalms. Ah, they have done a great deal for me, and I love those old psalms. English people laugh at them, and I believe there are some of our American friends who make themselves a little merry over them; but they are very close to the Hebrew, and there is a great deal of strength and beauty in their old rhythm. I used to say to my English friends, that the reason they did not like them was because they did not know how to read them; and I believe that is true of some of our American brethren. Just think of these four lines:

> "Their blood about Jerusalem
>   Like water they have shed,
> And there was none to bury them,
>   When they were slain and dead."

What a fine old ballad-like cadence there is in these lines! Then take these others:

> "The waters, Lord, perceived Thee,
> The waters saw Thee well,
> And they for fear aside did flee;
> The depths on trembling fell."

Where shall we find grander poetry than that? Or take that one that comes to me with the sound of trumpets and the trampling of horses, as a battle-cry:

> "In Judah's land God is well known,
> His name in Isr'el's great,
> In Salem is His tabernacle,
> In Zion is His seat.
> There arrows of the bow He brake,
> The shield, the sword, the war;
> More glorious Thou than hills of prey,
> More excellent art far."

Why, set me to singing that, and I would fight in any battle, and I do not wonder that the Covenanters conquered at Drumclog when they made their onset to the glorious sound of that martial song. I say that I am very sorry that these old songs are disappearing from among us. I like the psalms. I think it would have been better if they had not been pushed so much out by the hymns; and in my church, if we could not have the old Scottish psalms, which, perhaps, would be asking a little too much, I would rejoice to have the prose psalms chanted by the whole congregation. I think we have the right to sing with Cowper, Newton, Montgomery, Bonar, Lyte, and with Palmer and others here on this side of the Atlantic; but we must not forget David, the sweet singer of Israel. As an Old-Light minister once said to me, "There is nothing like a good hard psalm." I was preaching in his pulpit in the earlier years of my ministry, and I was going to give out a paraphrase, but when I turned to that part of the book I found its leaves stitched up, and at the close of the service I said to him, "Why have you got the paraphrases stitched up?" He said, "There is nothing like a good hard psalm." I said, "I have no fault to find with the psalms, but sometimes I like a paraphrase too." Occasionally even the precentors ventured on a similar protest. I remember a friend giving out a paraphrase, when he was preaching for a brother, and the man who was in the box did not make any attempt to open the book, so the preacher leaned over and said, "It is such and such a paraphrase." The precentor replied: "We don't sing paraphrases here, sir, but I will sing the same number of a psalm."

Now I am thankful to say that we have got rid of a great deal of that; but at the same time I don't think we have done well in so largely omitting the psalms from our books of praise, and I congratulate you in retaining so many of them in yours.

I have said a good deal more than I meant to say when I arose, but I may fitly bring my remarks to a close by quoting from the psalter, as my earnest prayer for you and my dear friend your pastor, the familiar words, " Peace be within thy walls and prosperity within thy palaces. For my brother and companion's sake, I will now say, Peace be within thee. Because of the house of the Lord my God, I will seek thy good." God bless you.

The Church in Thirty-fourth Street, West of Broadway.

Wednesday, October 28, 1885.—7.30 P. M.

THE SABBATH-SCHOOL MEETING.

The three Sabbath-Schools completely filled the body of the Church, and the galleries were thronged by parents and friends.

The Rev. John Spaulding, D. D., presided, and interesting addresses were made by the Revs. John Thomson, D. D., James D. Wilson, D. D., George Alexander, D. D., and Edward F. Parsons, M. D., a former Superintendent.

The exercises were varied by the singing of appropriate hymns by the children, and refreshments were served to them in the Lecture-room, at the close of a most enjoyable evening.

Many of the former officers and teachers were specially invited, and by their presence added greatly to the interest of the occasion.

Thursday, October 29, 1885.—7.30 P. M.

Reminiscences and Social Reunion.

After introductory devotional services, led by the
Rev. James White, D. D.,

Addresses were made by the

Rev. John Spaulding, D. D.
Rev. Andrew Shiland, D. D.
Rev. John Thomson, D. D.
Mr. Robert Carter.

Some fine solos were rendered by Miss Josie McPherson and Mr. Charles Renwick.

A sumptuous Collation was arranged in the Lecture-room, which had been elegantly fitted up for the Reunion. The intermingling of old and new members, the exchange of memories and hopes, congratulations and good wishes, protracted the large assembly until past the midnight.

ADDRESS

BY THE

Rev. John Spaulding, D. D.

THE ELOQUENCE OF AGE.

WHAT more instructive, more impressive, more elevating than the eloquence of age, when that age has been spent in the line of truth, duty, and usefulness! Especially when that age measures the life of a venerable church! Thus far this week we have listened, and been deeply moved by the eloquence of the pulpit; this evening we listen to the eloquence of the church, speaking from the pews, and giving reminiscences of a century.

Is it not written, "Days should speak, and multitude of years should teach wisdom"? Days should speak, because they have so much to say, and years should teach, because they have wisdom to impart from their accumulated stores of practical knowledge. Let, then, days and years express their strong emotions, so as to excite corresponding emotions in others. There is eloquence in the tones of their voice, in the force of their language, and in the depth of their impressions.

On the old homestead stands a venerable oak. It was an acorn when your grandfather, or father, was a boy. Every year has added a concentric circle to its growth till it now numbers five score. It has lifted its head high, and higher a hundred summers, and battled with the storms of a hundred winters. It sprang from its acorn-cell two years after the close of the Revolutionary War, and was only the size of a walking-cane when General Washington was inaugurated the first President of the United States. But now, strong in its roots, strong in limbs, and majestic in trunk, it stands the venerable and eloquent teacher of three and a half generations past, and many generations to come. We gather about the old oak as loving pupils salute an old teacher; as dutiful and dear children kiss the wrinkled cheeks of an aged parent.

That venerable oak is the emblem of this venerated Fourth Church.

To-day it is our privilege to gather in its courts, and feel the eloquence of its age. It was "built upon the foundation of the apostles and prophets, Jesus Christ himself being the chief corner-stone." On such a foundation there has been eloquence in its stability.

During these hundred years, how many *isms* have clamored for attention and recognition! — skepticism, socialism, communism, Arminianism, Socinianism, unitarianism, old-schoolism, new-schoolism, spiritism, higher criticism, lower gnosticism, and as many other *isms* as there are degrees of latitude between Cape Farewell and Cape Horn. But it has given place to them, by subjection, no, not for an hour. While to the Jews Christ crucified has been "a stumbling-block, and to the Greeks foolishness," to this church it has been the "wisdom of God, and the power of God." The old doctrines of the Bible, as imbedded in Christian experience, and formulated by the Westminster Assembly of divines, have ever been its substantial and satisfactory creed. So doctrinally and eloquently it has stood,

"Like some tall cliff, that lifts its awful form,
Swells from the vale, and midway leaves the storm;
While round its breast the rolling clouds are spread,
Eternal sunshine settles on its head."

And there has been eloquence in its unity.

Different as may have been its opinions on matters before it on various occasions, and earnest as may have been its discussions, the hour of decision has generally brought concession, concurrence, and a practical unity. Seldom has so long a chain had so few broken links. Its unity has been its past strength, and is to-day an eloquent pledge of growing strength with its increasing years.

And how eloquent has been its sympathy!

When one member has suffered, all the members have suffered with it; when there has been sickness in the family, how honest and earnest the inquiries! How suggestive and comforting the fragrant flowers or delicate token sent to the sick one! When death has drawn the sable curtains, and summoned to the funeral, how many have found it better to go to the house of mourning than to the house of feasting! In a city like this, where the black or white badge so often hangs from the knob of the door-bell, where the daily hearse is no stranger, and the indifferent multitude passes by with no care or inquiry about the departed, how kind and Christian is the sight of a house full of mourners! Such expressions of sympathy have characterized this old city congregation beyond any I have known. Eloquent tributes are they to the best feelings and consolations of human hearts.

And what shall we say of the eloquence of its charities and contributions? If they have not been so large and proud as some others, they have been perennial. If they have not been the babbling mountain brooks, dry more than half the year, they have been the silent flowing springs, keeping their banks verdant and fruitful the whole twelve months.

Its Benevolent Society, now ninety years old, has raised and expended for the relief and comfort of its worthy church members over $6000, while its estimated public and private charities have exceeded $720,000. Besides what it has given for other church edifices, it has recently built a Mission Chapel at an expense of $20,000, and this house of worship at a cost of $140,000. Thus, while it has cared for its own household, it has generously, may I not say eloquently, contributed to the welfare of others.

Then there is the outspoken eloquence of its pulpit during these ten decades. An average of two sermons on a Sabbath aggregates 10,400. What shall we say of the instructive, impressive, and persuasive power of these more than ten thousand sermons and other addresses adapted to various occasions! How many darkened minds have thereby been enlightened; how many sad hearts comforted; how many consciences quickened to the discernment of right and wrong; how many brought to the obedience of the truth, as it is in Jesus; how many feet turned from the broad into the narrow way; how many, now in heaven and on the way there, are enabled to say, through the eloquence of the truth uttered from this pulpit, by the grace of God we are what we are; all we now are, and all we hope to be!

And what of the about two hundred and fifty communion seasons during the ten decades of this church, where, from far and near, the tribes have come up, the tribes of the Lord, unto the testimony of Israel, to give thanks unto the name of the Lord! Is there nothing eloquent; nothing deeply emotional, and producing deep emotions; nothing strengthening the principles, motives, and purposes of faith; nothing sanctifying and molding character for usefulness and heaven in all these seasons of partaking the memorials of the broken body, and shed blood of the Lamb of God? Also in the some five thousand meetings for prayer and praise; where the "eyes of the Lord are upon the righteous, and His ears are open unto their cry"; whence the hands of faith have reached heaven, and brought down blessings to gladden both earth and heaven. Moreover, in the thousands of Bible-class and Sabbath-school lessons given the children and youth; is there no eloquence in the entrance of the words that give light and understanding to the simple? Ask Robert Raikes, who founded the institution of Sabbath-schools four years before this church was born, and who has been in heaven seventy-four years; ask the children and youth who have studied and learned these lessons under this roof-tree,—some of them are already in that bright world, and others are on the way there,—ask them whether there is anything enlightening, subduing, and saving in the words of Him who spake as never man spake?

> Our hearts rejoice, our bosoms glow:
> This hour, what cheering visions rise!
> These children, nurtured here below,
> Shall swell the assemblies of the skies!

Then, to crown all, the eloquence of the silent power, the unconscious influence, and the practical religion in the private lives of the pastors, officers, and members of this church.

Enoch's private walk with God in the presence of his contemporaries 300 years, and its influence 5000 years since God took him, speaks even more eloquently to-day than the public, excellent sacrifice of Abel. So with the piety of the men and women who have walked with God here. The dead yet speak. It is the still small voice that of old spake to the people through His prophet, and now speaks to us through His people. So much for this century oak. Such is the eloquence of its age. Eloquent in its stability; eloquent in its unity; eloquent in its sympathy; eloquent in its charities; eloquent in its sermons and public addresses; eloquent in its communion seasons; eloquent in its meetings for prayer; eloquent in its Bible-class and Sabbath-school instructions; eloquent in the godly lives of its pastors, officers, and members; eloquent in all these aspects, may this centennial oak live many centuries to come; like the Psalmist's tree planted by the rivers of water,

> Ever fruitful, ever fair,
> As any trees prospered where
> God created trees, and men,
> To make His grace and glory shine.

ADDRESS

BY THE

REV. ANDREW SHILAND, D. D.

ON Monday evening, listening to the eloquent addresses, I was greatly interested and delighted. Especially was I pleased with Dr. Hall's glowing description and analysis of the Scotch and Scotch-Irish character; and while enjoying his remarks, so excellent and so pertinent, I confess I felt a little elated that there was Scotch blood running through my veins, though of the second generation. I claim to be an American, and yet, strange as it may seem, I have sometimes been taken for a Scotchman or Scotch-Irishman.

Many, many years ago, when I preached for Dr. Stark in Grand street, shortly after leaving the Seminary, as I came down out of the pulpit, an old Scotch lady came up to me, took me by the hand most cordially, and said, "How do you do? I am so glad to see you. How long since you came over?"

Your worthy pastor requested me to give some recollections and reminiscences of Dr. Stark this evening. My knowledge of this church and my acquaintance with its leading members extends back more than a third of a century. Most of those men whom I knew long years since have gone to their reward. They have left the Church Militant for the Church Triumphant. Being dead, however, they yet speak, and their memory is still fresh in the minds of those who knew them. We cherish with gratitude the recollection of the excellency of their Christian character. They were noble-minded men, large-hearted, open-handed, liberal, and active in their support of the church and in their endeavors to advance the interests of Christ's cause and kingdom. I have known all the pastors of this church, from the time of Dr. Stark down to the present pastor.

My acquaintance with Dr. Stark goes back to my boyhood days, and I remember his appearance very well when I was a little boy. He used to visit Cambridge, and was called upon to assist the venerable Dr. Alexander Bullions at his communion. How often have I heard him there in that church on those memorable occasions, which I can never forget. My impressions of Dr. Stark at that time are as fresh now as at that very hour when I first saw him. His high forehead, his bright piercing eyes, his well-formed mouth and chin, indicative of decision and determination, and his pleasant face beaming with intelligence and benevolence, made their impression on my mind; and when I heard him in the pulpit preaching the word of God and at the communion table making his address, young as I was, I still retain a vivid remembrance of his sincerity, his deep earnestness and solemnity of manner. When I came to years of maturity and became connected with his family, I became acquainted with him not only as a minister of the Gospel, as a preacher, and in church courts and councils; I knew him also intimately in his own household, at his own fireside, as a husband and as a father.

Dr. Stark was a man of more than ordinary intellectual ability. No one could be in his presence and enjoy his conversation for any length of time without being impressed with the fact that he bore the unmistakable marks of a scholar and a Christian gentleman. By his learning, as well as by his natural gifts, he was fitted to honor any profession in life which he might have chosen. He had a wonderful skill, if I may so speak, in discerning men and discriminating character. He knew how to read men, how to manage men, and never at any time was he embarrassed or confused in any position in which he might be placed. I remember that, when I was a pastor in Philadelphia (and I may say here in this connection that he laid his hands upon me, with the other members of the clergy, when I was ordained, made the ordaining prayer and preached the sermon), he was summoned to Philadelphia as a witness in an important civil suit involving a large amount of church property. He was placed in the witness-chair, and the lawyer tried his best by cross-examination to confuse and embarrass him, and put question after question, so as to get him to answer the question just as he wanted it, to suit his side of the case; but Dr. Stark sat there in the witness-chair, perfectly composed, and answered the questions in a most courteous and dignified manner, and never for one single moment did that astute lawyer gain the advantage over his witness. After the trial was over, or at the close of this meeting, a lawyer present asked, "Who was that old gentleman who sat in the witness-chair, who proved himself too much for that lawyer?" "Oh, that was Dr. Stark, of New-York, the pastor of a Presbyterian church."

"What! he a minister?" said he. "Why, he never should have been a minister. He ought to have been a lawyer."

In the accuracy and extent of his learning, in the wide range of his reading, Dr. Stark had few superiors. In theology, in philosophy, in his knowledge of history and of poetry, both ancient and modern, he excelled. Indeed, he was heard to say to a friend of mine on one occasion, that if Homer's "Iliad" were blotted out of existence, he supposed he could restore the most of it from memory. In early life he had given his heart to God, and all his faculties and acquirements he consecrated to the service of Christ, used them for the service of his Lord and Master and the building up of His cause and kingdom in the world. As a preacher he was impressive and instructive. He made thorough preparation for the pulpit. He did not write out his sermons in full, it is true. I have a small volume of his sermons, six inches by four or five, and in that are contained the sermons of a whole year. The outlines of each sermon occupied about two pages of that small volume; but it was a matter of conscientious duty with him to go before his congregation with beaten oil. As a minister and as a pastor he was thoroughly furnished, and I never knew a more sincere, devout, and devoted minister of the gospel. He was a man, too, of wonderful wisdom and prudence. By this I mean that he seemed to know on every occasion just the right thing to say and do at the right time. To illustrate this, let me give you a little incident. In his congregation there was a woman who was considered, to say the least, a little queer, and some thought her a little crazy, although she was harmless. Dr. Stark, when he was preaching, often had his eyes upon the open Bible, and this queer old lady thought that he read his sermons. She had a great contempt for sermons read in the pulpit; but she couldn't find out whether he had his manuscript there and read it or not, and she was determined to know. Consequently, one Sabbath morning she went early and took her place in the pulpit, desiring to find out whether her pastor read his sermons from manuscript or not. When Dr. Stark came into the pulpit, he saw this woman sitting there, and said very quietly, "What are you doing here?" "Oh," said she, "I came up here to see if you read your sermons." Well, Dr. Stark didn't get into a furor and hustle her out or call for a policeman. Instead of that, he said to her very gently, "Well, ma'am, there is no need of us both being here. If you are going to stay here, I will go down." He reached to get his hat, and she shot out of that pulpit like an arrow, and he had no more trouble with that woman.

Let me say to you here, that the intelligence of his congregation, their knowledge of Christian doctrine, and their zeal in every good word and work, their adherence to the truth, their walking in the truth and doing all they could to disseminate the truth, were the best testimonials of the faithfulness of Dr. Stark as a preacher and minister of the gospel. Many a family in his congregation were made wiser, better, and richer for his judicious and prudent counsels. In his own family he was a model for household order and parental instruction. To instruct his children in the statutes and commandments of God, to have them thoroughly indoctrinated in the grand truths of the Bible, and to impress upon their minds and upon their hearts the blessed doctrines of the Gospel, he conceived to be of the utmost importance. And not only did he believe in this Bible, from Genesis to Revelation, but he believed in the Shorter Catechism, and he taught it to his children as long as he lived. And let me tell you, he took them through that catechism once every three weeks, taking one-third of it every Sabbath afternoon. Now some of you may think that this was altogether unnecessary. Some think nowadays that that Shorter Catechism is not, after all, of great consequence; but I maintain that it is the most compact expression of Christian doctrine to be found anywhere in the world,—a vade mecum of theology. Some people do not believe in teaching that catechism to small children, because they do not understand it. Well, if they do not understand it at the time, they will understand it afterward; and when it is impressed upon their minds early they do not forget it easily. A few years ago, when I was pastor at Mt. Kisco, Dr. S. Irenæus Prime, lately deceased, spent the Sabbath with me, preached for me in the morning, and talked to the Sunday-school in the afternoon; and in talking to the Sunday-school children he made this proposition: that he would give a beautiful gilt Bible to each one who would recite, without any mistake, the Fourth Commandment. Several of them volunteered to recite that Fourth Commandment, and they thought they knew it, but not one of them said it perfectly; they all left something out or put something in. Not one of them got the Bible. When he came back to the parsonage, my wife said to him: "Dr. Prime, I think I can repeat that commandment." He said, "I don't believe you can. Now, recite that Fourth Commandment, without putting in a word or leaving out a word, and I will give you a Bible." She began, and recited it *verbatim et literatim*,—did not leave out or put in a single word. Said he, "You shall have the Bible." When he went back to New-York he sent her the Bible, with his name on the fly-leaf.

Now that catechism was so thoroughly impressed on her mind by regular recitation when she was a child, that if she had lived to be as old as Methusaleh she could never forget it. So I can tell you, if you want to impress the catechism upon the minds of the children, teach them when they are young.

Dr. Stark never neglected the homes of the poor, and was a welcome guest wherever he went. Perhaps many of you, I do not know whether all of you, know that in 1849 he went to Scotland for his health; he had been laboring a long time, was very much run down, and it was thought that an ocean voyage and a visit to his native land would be beneficial. He was a guest of his cousin, Rev. Dr. Stark, of Dennyloanhead. None of his family thought him seriously ill when he left his home. While at Dr. Stark's, at Dennyloanhead, Scotland, he retired to rest and woke up in heaven. He was found dead in his bed, and it was observed by the members of the family that when he conducted family devotions that evening it was with unusual solemnity and impressiveness; he seemed to be at the very gate of heaven, and they all remembered the last prayer made by Dr. Stark on that night, just before his spirit ascended to the throne of God who gave it. There was mourning in his church and among his people when the sad news came of his death—

the bereavement was deeply lamented, from the oldest to the youngest member of his congregation. They felt it as they would feel the loss of a father. They laid his remains in Greenwood, and erected over the place where he sleeps a costly and beautiful monument to his memory.

And now, my dear friends and brethren, allow me, in conclusion, to congratulate you on this centennial of your church life. Although you have been so often congratulated as to this already, may I not also do the same? I congratulate you on having had, in succession, such able, such devoted, such pious and godly men to minister among you and to break to you the bread of life. I also commend you for the esteem, the respect, the affection, and the love which you have always manifested toward your pastors, from the very beginning, I believe, to the present hour. I commend you for this, and I congratulate you on having had your church work and your church life in this century of the world's history, the most eventful and fruitful of all the centuries, in discovery, in invention, in art, in science, in literature, in missionary work and enterprise, in aggressive and progressive Christianity; in short, in everything that pertains to the elevation and salvation of men. I congratulate you upon living in this time of such unspeakable blessings, of such unparalleled opportunities for getting and doing good. And let me say to you, do not be alarmed because of the great hue and cry nowadays about skepticism and infidelity. Do not be alarmed because there are those who talk against this blessed volume and tell you that it is becoming effete and worn out. Do not be alarmed because there are those who tell you that Christianity is declining, and the ancient faith is becoming decrepit and soon will disappear. I tell you there is nothing of the kind. There was never so much Christianity in the world as to-day. There never were so many followers of the Lord Jesus Christ as to-day. Why, a hundred years ago there was only one church member, or professor of Christianity, to fourteen; and in 1880 there was one professing Christian, or church member, to five. Do not be alarmed, I say, for all this talk of infidelity and skepticism. There are to-day six millions of Sunday-school children, and do you not think, with these six millions of Sunday-school children, and with all the professed followers of the Lord Jesus Christ, we shall be able to triumph over the world, the flesh, and the devil? I think we will. Do not be alarmed, and do not think infidelity is going to triumph, when there are at least eight or ten churches of the different denominations of Christians, taking them altogether, erected for every day of the year. Their spires and their towers point heavenward, inviting men to the house of prayer, directing them to the many mansions of rest and of glory.

And now, in the language of the apostle, I beseech you, brethren, that you increase more and more as a church, as individuals, increase more and more in your faith, in your knowledge, in your piety, in your self-consecration to Christ, and in every good word and work. Be of good comfort, be of one mind; live in peace, and the God of love and peace shall be with you. Amen.

ADDRESS

BY THE

REV. JOHN THOMSON, D. D.

MY DEAR FRIENDS: I think it is a good thing for me that the clock points a little beyond the time appointed for the refection so kindly provided for us in the lecture-room. This hour has very pleasantly and profitably passed; indeed, in such a way as to lead me to think that it is not within my power to add anything to the reminiscences of those dear brethren to whom you have been listening. I cannot, at this late hour, go back to other holy memories, but I may, in a sentence or two, put some of my brethren in mind of how and when I came to be pastor of this church and successor to that worthy and excellent man, the Rev.

Dr. Andrew Stark. I had come from a poor provincial city, on what I may call a privateering expedition to rich New-York, of which expedition I may just say this, that it was successful. Good Robert Carter, on the platform beside me to-night, had heard me conduct the service at the weekly prayer-meeting in the Scotch Church here, and he knew my errand. He was applied to at a late hour on the Saturday evening for supply for the Associate Presbyterian Church in Grand street for the following day. I happened to be sojourning in what is now, I believe, or was then, West Washington Place; and between nine and ten o'clock that night one of the elders, on his suggestion, called and asked me whether I would meet the congregation on the following day. He told me nothing about any specialty in the occasion, and nothing about the people; but it was, nevertheless, a day of deepest and saddest interest to them, for during the preceding week the remains of their beloved pastor and spiritual father had been brought from Dennyloanhead, in Scotland, to New-York, and laid in their final resting-place in Greenwood. Having consented to occupy the pulpit, I found that a number of the members of the church were comforted exceedingly by the message which, in total ignorance of their circumstances, I had received of the Lord for them. The words of my text were: "Sing ye to her a vineyard of red wine. I the Lord do keep it; I will water it every moment; lest any should hurt it, I will keep it night and day." The theme was God's care of and interest in the prosperity and peace of His people. Well, very soon thereafter, early in the spring of 1850, an invitation was sent to me to become their pastor. I could not, however, see it to be my duty to accept it, for the congregation to which I was ministering in the city of St. John's, New Brunswick, was a recently organized one, and not as yet strong or vigorous. The congregation in New-York were, I had reason to believe, vexed and disturbed by my refusal; but only for a season, for at the close of a year they renewed the invitation, which, after consultation with friends, and prayer to our Heavenly Father, I accepted. The condition of the church at that time was fine; men of shrewdness and probity managed its finances, and men of deep piety superintended its spiritual concerns. They were ready to welcome a leader among them, and they did give me a hearty welcome, and I entered upon the charge full of hope. Throughout all the years that succeeded, I have no recollection of any dark shadow resting upon us, so far as their interest in me and my work as God's servant was concerned — not one. We met inwardly. Those years passed in mutual affection, which showed itself then and shows itself now. They attended the ordinances of God's house with regularity, and manifested the spirit of true piety in their outward lives, and in their homes. I remember no instance in which I could not approach any one of their families with the fullest, heartiest consent on both sides. They were to me, mine; and I was to them, theirs. Many of you remember the old church at the corner of Grand and Mercer streets. Many a time I have gone over that church, when far distant from it, in thought, and even with quickened vision, tracing every occupant of every pew from the front of the pulpit to the door, knowing full well that if still alive in the providence of God, they were there on that day in their accustomed places, from the youngest to the oldest, worshiping the God of their fathers with all the piety and steadfast adherence to our simple forms of worship which they had learned from their fathers and rejoiced to maintain. The elders of that time were earnest men, and men of profound piety and sound common sense. Of one of them in particular it was wont to be said by those who knew him intimately: "William Boyd is an elder that rules well, and nobody knows it"; and of another, "In none of our churches is there a more Nathaniel-like man than James Chalmers." These were typical men in our session; their brethren were like them, though not to the same degree—

"diversities of gifts, but the same spirit." Of two others it was my privilege to watch the spiritual growth, and to give God thanks for what He was pleased to work both in and by them, both in and for the church. John Aitken was a man whom God greatly blessed, and not the least in this, that He was pleased to make him a blessing. In like manner was it with David Irwin, and James Stuart, and Edward Mackenzie, and Joseph Paterson, and William Whitewright.

As to the trustees of the church, I can only say of them all, that they were men "who feared God and hated covetousness." They were God's men. Only one of them survives now; the others have gone home; and in their track my dear old friend David Morrison follows hard. Yet he is spared to us all, and with his soul and strength and mind more strongly devoted than ever to the best interests of our Zion. And having mentioned these, I cannot but mention two others, one in the eldership, and one on the Board of Trustees,— James and Joseph Stuart, whom all Christian men who knew them esteemed very highly in love for their works' sake. I know you will join with me when I say, that to no four men in the church have we been so largely indebted as to John Aitken, David Irwin, and James and Joseph Stuart. Of these it may be truly said, that "they have done exploits." On two occasions I was personally a witness to their liberality: First, when the Mission-house in Thirty-third street was opened for home missionary work, very largely at their expense; and second, when, a few years before that, this magnificent edifice was dedicated to the service of God, and a sum of $40,000, in addition to the sum then in the hands of the Board of Trustees, was required and was subscribed in the course of one week, that it might be opened and dedicated free of debt. We were prosperous in those days, and our prosperity has continued unto this day. There are those around me to-night who will attest what I say, that additions of thirty, forty, and on one occasion over sixty, were at communion seasons made to the church.

In 1861 it was my duty to sever my connection with the church. It was a trying season not less to the church than to myself. Yet during the three succeeding years our intercourse as friends and brethren suffered no interruption. To join the young in holy wedlock, and to baptize the children of those to whom I had ministered, my presence and services were frequently required. These and other proofs of holiest interest show the feeling of unity and love in the divine fellowship that continued to follow me even after I had relinquished the formal charge of this church, and that only reached maturity when the old pastoral tie was once more formed and blessed for added years.

A second time the pastoral tie had to be loosed, and now about eleven years have passed since that time. Ten of these I have spent in my native land. Often, oh, how often my heart goes back to the scenes of my earlier ministry, and to you, my dear youth, whom I left as children,— I dare not tell you how fondly loved,— and whom I now find, instead of your fathers and mothers, walking still in their fellowship, and in living communion with God; and to you, my beloved brethren and sisters who yet survive, and who, bearing the burden of a few more years, and a few more heavy crosses, rendered all the more heavy for want of that stronger arm on which you were wont to lean, or that more gentle heart in unison with which you passed along the checkered valley, no fears dividing you, and no alarms creating distrust between you, and now looking forward in hope to be united with them again, when He shall appear "to be glorified in His saints, and to be admired in all them that believe." Of many a token of your continued affection have you made me during these last years the recipient. Each returning season has been made by your kindness to minister to my comfort, and to that of my family; and now, as if to crown my warmest wishes, you have made me and my daughter partakers with you in these grand and successful services. The only regret is the absence of her whom, next to the supreme gift of the Lord Jesus our Saviour and Redeemer, I gladly hail as the light of our humble mountain home, and as the desire of my heart. In spirit I know she is with us here to-night, and sustained by her prayers, and strong in the grace of our one ever-living Head, and resolved on continuing through His grace even to the end, as being heirs together of the grace of life. I offer you, old and young, her love and ever fond regards for you all.

With these few pleasing reminiscences I have already taken up too much of your time, so let me only say that, God willing, I shall carry with me to my dying day the ever sweet recollection that I have been once more by your generous kindness in the midst of my old flock. Yet I cannot stop here. For I see many of God's witnesses before me, whom, though not associated with my earlier pastorate, I should yet be a most ungrateful man not to recognize as very dear to me, because now joined as friends and brethren to my friends and brethren, and as such joined also to me; and without formally naming you all, let me select a few who have been known to me for a longer time than the others, many of such the followers or successors of those who were my first acquaintances and brethren in this dear hundred-year-old church. Few of you, I am sure, will be surprised when I mention the name of one dear old friend of yours and mine who, ever since his connection with this church, has proved himself a right trusty and most earnest friend; who has laid us all under a heavy bond of obligation by the consecration of himself and his large experience in the Lord's vineyard to our service in the Lord. Of course, I can but mean the Rev. Dr. John Spaulding, whose gifts and graces are the crown of a long and venerable age. I do not need to commend you, beloved friends, to his great prayers. I know they rise before the Lord daily for you, and I know that I join you in the responding prayer on behalf both of that dear good man and his venerable wife, that the God of the covenant may bless him still more and more abundantly, and continue His work in him and by him to His church, both by sea and land, till, ripe and ready for the better land, he shall welcome the approach of the voice that shall summon a willing son to its fullness of joy and everlasting delight.

And only one other will I name now, because I have long known him, even from the first years of my residence in this city. I can see him in his early manhood with his young wife in their seats in the old church at the corner of Mercer street. I can trace his career from one position to another — never ambitious, save to do in every duty only and always the right; the fear of the Lord ever before his eyes, and the love of God in his heart — sometimes sorely tried alike in his personal and family life, yet never overborne by the strokes of his Father's rod, and ever disposed to glorify God even in the fires that eternal love so often kindles for the fuller purification of God's elect. So has my early friend, and I can add my tried friend, Archibald McLintock, an elder in our beloved church, grown during these last thirty years. The honest, modest youth of nearly thirty years ago, under the mighty blessing of the living God, has grown to be what I believe he will continue to be — a faithful witness of the Lord Jesus, alike in joy and in sorrow, and to all young men a steady compass, by the aid of which they may shape their course alike through the entanglements and temptations of youth and the trials of manhood.

And now with one other name I close these truthful but desultory remarks. I commend to your prayers my beloved friend and successor in the ministry of the Fourth Church, the Rev. Joseph R. Kerr, whom may the Lord continue long to strengthen and support in his arduous though much-loved work. He and I have not often met; indeed, but twice — once for a few brief and hurried hours in Scotland, and again here in New-York, for a few too brief but most pleasant weeks. Having heard much about him, I esteemed him before I saw him; and now that I have seen and heard from his pulpit and amid the sanctities of his home, I have come to "esteem him very highly in love for his work's sake." I trust you will endeavor to cheer and encourage him by your diligent attendance on the services which I know it is his heart and his life to conduct. And now I must really stop, for the hour is late.

ADDRESS

<small>BY</small>

MR. ROBERT CARTER.

DEAR FRIENDS: At this late hour it would be very improper for me to spend five minutes in addressing you. I have felt a deep interest in this church for fifty-four years and more. I have watched pastors and people; many of them I have accompanied to the river side and bade them an affectionate farewell. I have seen the power of divine grace by the dying bed of, oh, how many who occupied the pews in this church. The first person I took by the hand when I reached this city on the 16th of May, 1831, was a member of this church, and he stood by me for more than forty years. The pastor of this church at that time, to whom I had a letter of introduction, received me as a son who had come back after a long absence. I owed a debt to that good man, and came expecting to pay it, however feebly; but I cannot do it now. He is yonder, and, oh, how many whom I loved so dearly are with him. Oh, my brethren, it is a thin veil that separates the seen from the unseen world. We long with heart-sickness and home-sickness to see these dear brethren that left us and went on to their reward. I thought I should say something about the great work they did, but I cannot do it tonight, my dear friends. In a little while I shall step across that stream that separates this world from the next; and, oh, what a scene it will be, when those whom I love so well and who did so much to help me on in my humble work shall appear in glory, their robes washed in the blood of the Lamb, singing the praises of our Father in heaven forever and forever. God bless you all and keep you all, make you true followers of those who through faith and patience are inheriting the promises; carry you safely through the storms and tempests of this narrow world; and when the night comes to which there shall be no morning, then may the everlasting arms be underneath you and an entrance be administered into the glories of our Father's house. Amen.

Mr. Carter has kindly furnished the following reminiscences:

NEW-YORK, Oct. 30, 1885.

Rev. Dr. Kerr.

DEAR SIR: Fifty years ago I became acquainted with a member of your church in whom I felt a deep interest. He was a native of Banff, in the north of Scotland, and in early life emigrated to New-York. He was industrious, economical, and acquired some property, but the clouds gathered over him. He lost his property, his wife and his children. Broken in health and crushed in spirit he struggled heavily on. After some time he became almoner of the St. Andrew's Society, and there his Christian character developed wonderfully. He was one of my constant visitors. He filled his pockets with the "Crook in the Lot," and other good books, and dropped one here and another there. He counseled the sick and prayed with them. He often caused the widow's heart to ring for joy. But his strength gave way, and he came to me and said, "I feel I cannot do as I have done. I must give up my work. I have three sisters in my old home whom I have not seen for fifty years. I want to go to them — will you lend me the money I need?" I agreed, but after he left me I called upon some of the liberal members of the society and three thousand dollars were raised and invested by the president for his behoof. He reached his native village on a beautiful summer day. The doors of most of the cottages were open, and many of the women and children were seated outside enjoying the balmy air. He came to his own door and walked in. The arm-chair, where his father sat long ago, was empty, and he sat down in it. Three gray-haired maidens were sewing, and none spoke. After a little he looked at one and asked, "Are you Janet?" "Aye," was the answer. Again he asked another, "Are you Mary?" "Aye." And a third, "Are you Elizabeth?" "Aye." The wonder grew. At last one hastily rose and said, "Are you John?" "I am." The three seized him, and held him in close embrace. "Will you stay with us?" "By the help of God, I will. We shall live together, and when we die we shall sleep together in our old grave-yard."

A friend of mine visited him when he was nearing the Jordan. His end was peace. The everlasting arms were underneath him. May our last end be like his.

Yours affectionately,
Robert Carter.

Sacramental Hours.

Friday, October 30, 1885, at 7.30 P. M., the Preparatory Communion Service was held. Prayer was offered by the Rev. Erskine N. White, D. D., Moderator of the Presbytery of New-York; and the Rev. S. M. Hamilton, D. D., preached an impressive sermon from the text, John v. 1–9, "The Impotent Man at the Pool of Bethesda."

At a meeting of the Session, fourteen new members were welcomed into church fellowship.

On the following Sabbath morning the Rev. John Thomson, D. D., delivered an able discourse upon "The Bread of Life." In the afternoon, at four o'clock, a great congregation gathered for the celebration of The Lord's Supper, many persons coming from a distance to participate once more in the Communion as administered in the old home church.

Hearts melted and eyes overflowed as the one hundred and third Psalm was sung, in the Scotch version, without the organ accompaniment. The tune was "Balerma," and the Past came softly down through the familiar stanzas and the tender addresses of Rev. Drs. Thomson, Spaulding, and the Pastor, awakening fresh affection and trust toward that Saviour who is the same yesterday, to-day, and forever.

The benediction dismissed more than one communicant who felt that such a season could never come again this side of heaven.

THE NEW YORK
PUBLIC LIBRARY

ASTOR, LENOX AND
TILDEN FOUNDATIONS.

The West Side Chapel. 439 West Thirty-third Street.

The Covenant of the Praying Society

OUT OF WHICH THE CHURCH GREW.

NEW-YORK, JULY 4TH, 1779.

WE, the under-subscribers, taking into serious consideration the great loss our souls sustain by being, in adorable providence, deprived of the stated ordinances of the gospel in a witnessing way, for the glory of God, and the mutual advantage of our spiritual interests, have agreed to form ourselves into a praying society, according as we are warranted and commanded by the word of God. *Heb.* 10 & 23. 24. 25, "*Let us hold fast the profession of our faith without wavering: and let us consider one another, to provoke unto love, and to good works: not forsaking the assembling of ourselves together, as the manner of some is,*" &c. And as we are commanded by the precept; so we are encouraged by the promise of the Lord's presence being with us: As also, by the example of the saints of old. *Mal.* 3 & 16,

"*Then they that fear the Lord spake often one to another: and the Lord hearkened, and heard it: and a book of remembrance was written before him for them that fear the Lord, and that thought upon his name.*" As likewise the dispensations of providence, at this day, call loudly upon us to consider our wayes and to turn unto the Lord, with weeping and with supplication, pleading for, and believing that he will yet return again and have compassion upon us, and cast all our sins into the depths of the sea.

As it will be more for our mutual good and advantage to be of one heart and one way in the matters of the Lord; we have concluded to draw up a short specimen of our principles and the rules of this Society.

First. That none can be admitted into this Society but such as believe the word of God to be the only rule of faith and practice; and profess an adherence to the Reformation standards of the Church of Scotland contained in our confessions of faith, Larger and Shorter catechisms, The Presbyterian form of Church Government, worship, and discipline, as it was received, approved, and established by the foresaid Church of Scotland, betwixt the years 1638 & 1642; witnessed for in the secession testimony and the acknowledgment of sins prefixed to the bond for renewing our solemn covenants, to which we all profess an adherence.

Second. That no person lying under any scandal, without acknowledging the sin thereof, can be admitted as a member of this Society.

Third. That as the strong ought to bear the infirmities of the weak, and not to please themselves, so no member is to go before another, but every one is to go about duty as it comes his turn; and in our mutual conferences every one is to speak his mind freely, and those who have any scruples, with respect to what any member of the Society hath said or done, shall faithfully lay such scruples before the meeting, that they may be satisfied thereabout. In this way studying to agree together, that our prayers be not hindered.

Fourth. That all carnal and worldly discourses are to be avoided. When met together, we are to consider ourselves in the presence of God; who is at all times our witness, and will, in a little, be our impartial and unerring Judge. And in this, as in all other things, we will study to have a single eye to his glory.

Fifth. That curious speculations, and debates, about points of religion, are to be avoided as much as possible. That each member is to study the spiritual advantage of the others; our furtherance in the wayes of God, and in the knowledge and love of his truth, and of a testimony thereto, in this Day of awful Back Sliding.

Sixth. That we shall meet at such a place as we can agree upon and continue so long as we think will serve the purpose of edification.

Seventh. That no member is to absent himself from the meeting without a sufficient reason, which he is to satisfy the meeting after his return.

May the Lord, who, in a way of righteous Judgment, scattered our Israel, gather him again as a shepherd doth his flock: and Oh may the cause of truth and reformation obtain the ascendancy over all opposing interests in Britain, Ireland, and America, and throughout the world! and may all the publick commotions of the day be over-ruled for this end. Oh may the promise be remembered in our behalf, and in behalf of God's work-servants and people, in the aforesaid places! viz., "*As thy dayes so shall thy strength be.*"

Lastly. As it has been our lot to fall in evil Dayes, in which the Lord, in the way of a righteous judgment, has scattered us, as to our church state, in consequence of which, through the tumult, hurry, and confusion of the day, we all, or some of us, may, through inadvertancy, weakness or fear, have formerly, or of late, been left to fall, in regard to that holy, humble, circumspect and tender regard that allwayes ought to influence every part of our conduct; such as rash connections, engaged to by oath, inconsistent with our duty to God, to our neighbor, or ourselves, or by concessions of this kind, inconsistent with former ones, opposing oath to oath. As this is a prevailing evil, that obtains according to the different aspect of the times, we would desire to be helped, to have an eye to it, as a publick evil, to be mourned over, and particularly in forming our praying Society, to see how far any or all of these, or any other evil, mentioned or implied, are chargeable on any or all of us. And to be humbled before God on account of our untenderness, and endeavoring, through grace, jointly, for one another, as it were, with the finger on the sore, to betake ourselves to the blood of sprinkling.

This, for our mutual satisfaction, we unanimously profess, and, as an evidence of our sincerity, as there may be matter of scandal, unknown to us, since the dissolution of our church state, in this place, each of us, for ourselves, profess a willingness to submit to the Discipline of competent judiciary of the Lord's house (uniting, through grace, at maintaining our witnessing profession), on condition of the above supposed case. And it is in this spirit, and under these engagements, we consent to hold communion with one another as a praying Society.

In consequence of which we subscribe ourselves.

JOHN MCFARLAND.	JOHN MCALLISTER.
GEORGE GOSMAN.	ANDREW WRIGHT.
JAMES CRAIG.	ROBERT GOSMAN.

HYMNS.

These original hymns were prepared and presented by the Rev. John Spaulding, D. D., and were effectively interspersed through the several services.

> The memories of an hundred years,
> Awake our joys, and start our tears;
> As once more at the mercy seat,
> For praise and prayer we gladly meet.
>
> Meet us, our Father, make us prove,
> Thy faithfulness, and deathless love;
> So that with conscious sins forgiven,
> This day may be a pledge of heaven.
>
> Let memories of beloved gone,
> To sing and shine before thy throne;
> Be prompters to us waiting here,
> To share their songs and glory there.

Long may this church securely stand,
A beacon-light for sea and land,
A living bulwark for the truth,
To safely guide both age and youth.

Precious mem'ries cluster here,
Where they met for praise and prayer;
Where our fathers worshipped God,
Found, and kept the heavenly road.

Here an hundred years ago,
Springs of life began to flow;
Many centuries to come,
May the living waters run.

Blessed be the God of love,
For the rest of those above;
Blessed be the God of grace,
That we there may find a place.

Bright in hope and strong in faith,
May we keep the narrow path;
Till united there we sing,
Higher praises to our King.

O God, our fathers' God, and Friend,
  On us thy grace bestow;—
The blessing, thou didst give to them,
  An hundred years ago.

O come, thou quickening Spirit, come,
  And make our graces grow ;
Us sanctify, as thou didst them,
  An hundred years ago.

Praise God for memories of his love,
  For all enjoyed below;
Praise Him, and ne'er forget above,
  An hundred years ago.

———

Our Fathers sowed for us to reap,
  The harvests of to-day ;
And now their grateful children keep
  Their hallowed memory ;
We'll hold that memory ever dear,
  Till we, supremely blest,
Shall glorious in heaven appear,
  To share the final rest.

And while we gather up the sheaves,
  To shout the Harvest home,
A hand divine for each one wreathes
  A never-fading crown ;
A radiant crown of endless joy,
  And pledge of royal power,
Where saints and angels robed in white,
  Reign victors ever more.

Thanks to our God for daily bread,
  By Him so kindly given ;
Our manna on the thorny road,
  Up to the highest heaven :

Sweet comfort to us all the way,
   To that most blessed home,
Until we hear our Father say,
   Come, ransomed children, come!

Let days and years their lessons teach,
   In their incessant flow;
And in the retrospect now reach,
   An hundred years ago.

O God, let every setting sun,
   With bright and brighter glow,
Cheer on the work so well begun,
   An hundred years ago.

May children's children keep in mind,
   God's promise on the bow;
And with the present always blend,
   An hundred years ago.

Our fathers sowed full hopeful,
   That we should rise and reap
The harvest, and be faithful,
   And bright their mem'ry keep:
So gratefully we gather,
   The golden sheaves to-day;
And joyful come together,
   To bless their memory.

To God we are indebted,
    For all we now enjoy;
And all to be expected,
    In his divine employ;
To Him let praise and glory,
    Ever be gladly given,
And let the old, old story,
    Be ever new in heaven.

There, children in full chorus,
    Shall sing in sweetest song;
Praises to Him who saved us,
    And made our weakness strong.
To Him whose word enlightens,
    And cheers our upward way;
Whose very presence brightens,
    Our everlasting day.

BLESSED memories bright and clear,
    Cheer and help us waiting here;
Better when our work is done,
    Far beyond the setting sun.

God of life, of light, and love,
    Let our sweet experience prove
The rich fullness of thy grace,
    Till in heaven we take our place.

There with loved ones gone before,
    Shall we meet to part no more;
There with angels join to sing,
    Praises to our God and King.

LETTERS.

The following letter is from Mr. George H. Stuart, President of the Merchants' National Bank of Philadelphia, Pa., and formerly President of the U. S. Christian Commission.

Clifton Springs, N. Y.,
October 27, 1885.

Rev. Jos. R. Kerr, D. D.

My Dear Brother: When I accepted your kind invitation to be present and speak at the centennial celebration of your church, I hoped and expected to be so far recovered as to be able to do so; but, not being able, I write this brief note to say how sadly disappointed I am at having to miss participating in so interesting an occasion.

I had looked forward with much pleasure to greeting once again Rev. Dr. Thomson, of Scotland, one of your illustrious predecessors, with whom it was my privilege to hold a warm personal friendship.

I feel a deep interest in the earlier history of the church. It may interest some of the older members of the congregation to know that fifty-four years ago, as a boy, I attended your church with my oldest brother, John. During the fall, winter, and spring of 1831 and '32, while the cholera was in New-York, I boarded at the corner of John and Pearl streets, and twice each Sabbath day walked to the old church on Mercer street, which was then considered away up town. Your present location was then farm-lands.

The pew that I occupied was five from the front on the right-hand side of the aisle next Broadway. Very well do I remember the old pastor's familiar face, Rev. Dr. Stark; the peculiar shake of his head and trembling of the eye, as he gave out the familiar old Psalms of David. I recall many precious Sabbaths, and the impressions then made have followed me and helped shape and mold my Christian character. Since those days, I have retained a deep interest in the old church in which were spent so pleasantly the Sabbath days of my boyhood, the teachings of which have ever remained with me. My brothers James and Joseph subsequently for many years were members and officers of the congregation, and died in its communion, thus increasing my love for the old church.

It has come to my mind that the beloved pastor of your church in 1854 (Dr. Thomson) entertained at his house that eminent missionary of the gospel, the Rev. Dr. Alexander Duff, whom I had the privilege of inviting to our country, and that was the first house he slept in in America, and your church was the *first* one he preached in in New-York, and the *last* one he spoke in at that memorable parting meeting on the morning he left our shores. On the Sabbath when he preached *every foot* of room in the old Grand street church was occupied. My seat was at the foot of the pulpit, near one of the reporters, who had, during one of the Doctor's bursts of eloquence, laid down his pen, at which I reminded him that we wanted the sermon *fully* reported; and I shall never forget the rebuke he gave me when he said, "I must hear that man for *myself*." Those who were permitted to hear the now sainted Duff will recall his visit to your church as an occasion of much more than ordinary interest.

I remember very pleasantly that partly through my instrumentality you were called to the pastorate of the old church, and very greatly have I rejoiced over the success that has attended your ministry, and the continued and growing prosperity of the church under your kindly care.

In view of these facts, you will see how great a self-denial it is to me that I am not privileged to attend these meetings.

I trust and pray that the blessing of God may follow these special services and continue abundantly to bless you and the old church.

Fraternally yours in Christ,
Geo. H. Stuart.

The next letter is from Mr. James Robertson, of London, England, President of the Aldenham Institute, and Superintendent of the Mission Schools connected with the Regent Square Presbyterian Church.

21 Berners Street, London, W.,
October, 1885.

Dear Brethren: When I had the pleasure of seeing your beloved pastor here a few weeks ago, he extended to me a cordial invitation to be present at the centenary celebration of the Fourth Presbyterian Church, in the closing week of this month.

Few things would have given me more real pleasure, had it been possible for me to go. But, though necessarily absent in person, I shall be with you in spirit, and shall mingle my rejoicing and thanksgiving with those of the assembled congregation, in view of the fact that the Fourth Church has been for a hundred years a shining light, distributing with no stinted measure the glorious sunshine of the gospel of Jesus Christ.

An occasion such as this invites you to examine the record of these hundred years, both for the interest that such an examination possesses in itself, and that the experience of the past may serve to stimulate you to more entire consecration to the Master's service in the future.

My treacherous memory covers but a very short period of the century, as it was only in 1866 that my name was added to the roll, and I had the pleasure of being associated with you in church fellowship for not more than ten years.

It may be of interest, however, to recall that during these years the congregation took three most important steps, all of which indicated the progressive spirit which should characterize all Christian congregations. I refer first to the removal of the congregation to your present place of worship, which will doubtless be fittingly referred to in the *résumé* of the church's history you will have the pleasure of listening to.

The second important step was the introduction of the organ so long delayed out of proper regard for the opinion of those who could not view such a step as other than a retrograde one, but which I am glad to know has proved to be a real blessing because helpful in making the service of praise to be more perfectly and more heartily rendered.

The third important step was the starting of the West Side Mission, which resulted from a meeting of young men called by our esteemed pastor, the Rev. Dr. Thomson, for the express purpose of endeavoring to originate some sphere of Christian activity in which the young energies of the congregation might profitably find an outlet. It is pleasing to know that this mission still exists, and that it has been instrumental in fulfilling to a large extent the object of its existence.

Among the memories affecting me personally, I shall never forget with what reluctance I diffidently assumed the charge of a young men's Bible-class at the urgent solicitation of Dr. Thomson, and how much pleasure I afterward found in conducting it, though ever conscious of the imperfect manner in which that duty was performed.

Nor shall I cease to remember the impressive occasion when in 1870 I was one of six who, after having been duly elected by the congregation, were solemnly ordained to the office of the eldership.

Neither can I forget the indulgence and forbearance extended to me, both by the office-bearers of the church and my fellow-workers at the mission, during the years I ventured, without experience and in much weakness, to superintend the work at the West Side Mission.

I have alluded to these personal reminiscences because I feel sure there are many in the congregation in whose minds they will stir memories that perhaps have been long dormant. There is not one of them I am not thankful for, and I am free to acknowledge that the experience I gained by them has in some measure fitted, or at least helped me to a better performance of duty than otherwise would have been possible in the much wider sphere of church work in which I now find myself engaged.

The years referred to bring back to the mind's vision the holy men who were then the leaders of the congregation, namely: Mr. Whitewright, Mr. McKenzie, Mr. Allan, Mr. Aitken, Mr. Kydd, Mr. James Morrison, James and Joseph Stuart. What memories cluster round each name! I could fill pages of detail about them; this, however, would obviously be out of place in a communication of this character.

May God bless the Fourth Presbyterian Church. May you enter on your second century resolved that you will be more *His* than you have ever been, and though none of you can be present at the celebration of the second centenary, you can leave behind you such a record of personal holiness, Christian faith, and Christian activity as shall command the admiration of the generation to come, and serve as a pattern through the whole future history of the congregation. Believe me, dear brethren,

Yours in the bonds of Christian love,

JAMES ROBERTSON.

The following is from Robert Donald, Esq., Provost of Dunfermline, Scotland.

CITY CHAMBERS, DUNFERMLINE,
26 September, 1885.

Rev. Joseph Kerr, D. D., New-York.

MY DEAR SIR: I trust you have arrived home safe and well, much improved in health by your tour on this side of the Atlantic, and ready for the celebration of the centennial of the church endeared to you and me by many hallowed associations. I think the centennial of the Fourth Presbyterian Church of New-York really began to be celebrated when Mr. Thomas Kirkpatrick and I met you in Edinburgh last month. We were verily a circle of antiquaries when we sat down to dinner on that memorable day. Our lively little dinner-party augured well for the success of the Great Day of the Feast drawing near. Your centennial presence was decidedly patriarchal, with your son Joseph alongside of us. On your right hand you had Mr. George Robertson, whose position under the Crown here is custodian of the Palace and Abbey of Dunfermline. The Abbey is connected with the parish church. It was founded in 1070 by Queen Margaret, wife of Malcolm, King of Scotland, all of which is illustrated in a large window in the parish church, designed by Sir Noel Paton, and it is the most costly window in Scotland. On your left hand was Dr. Munro, of Kilmarnock, author of the antiquarian book, *Lake Dwellings of Scotland*. He and I went that day on a pilgrimage to some newly-discovered tombs of prehistoric Scotchmen. We handled the ashes and the urns of the Stone period of our country. Surely all this was prophetic of the centennial day approaching. In the midst of such gentlemen and such grand old buildings and such relics of antiquity, a hundred years seem of small account; but, for all that, the centennial of your church is a most important event to you and me. We say with the Psalmist, "A day in thy courts is better than a thousand," etc., etc.

I was admitted a member of the old Grand Street Church in the year of our Lord 1856, and well remember the good old times under the ministry of the Rev. Dr. John Thomson, our dear old friend, and the other standard-bearers in the church of those days, who were "able men, such as fear God,—men of truth." As one after another of them was removed, the more anxious minds of the church were often afraid others might not be found ready and willing to fill up the breaches; but a kind Providence brought forward men who by their prayers, their money, and their influence maintained the integrity and efficiency of the church now prospering under your own good ministry.

I trust you and those engaged with you in the work of the church may be blessed in your work.

With best wishes and kindest regards for you and yours, I remain, Yours faithfully,

ROBERT DONALD.

P. S. Herewith is a draft for one hundred dollars in behalf of centennial expenses.— R. D.

The Rev. Henry C. Cronin, the first missionary in charge of the West Side Chapel, writes:

PARSONAGE, SECOND CONGREGATIONAL CHURCH,
HAMILTON, N. Y., October 23d, 1885.

Mr. John H. Allen, 69 Seventh Avenue, New-York.

MY DEAR FRIEND: I received to-day, addressed in your handwriting, an invitation to attend the centennial services of the Fourth Presbyterian Church, for which please accept my thanks.

I regret that, owing to my church work and to sickness in my family, I shall be deprived the pleasure of being in attendance upon what will doubtless be very interesting and delightful services.

The receipt of your invitation brings up many memories of the past in connection with the Fourth Church and its Mission; of how the Lord led us and cared for us, and was better to us than our fears. I congratulate you and the church, with its pastor, upon the past, the present, and the outlook for the future, and pray that that future may prove more glorious than the past;

that the candlestick may never be removed out of its place, but that you who are the church of to-day, and they who shall be the church of the future, may see her " A quiet habitation — a tabernacle that shall not be taken down ; that not one of her stakes shall ever be removed, neither shall any of the cords thereof be broken."

If you shall have opportunity, please remember me kindly to Drs. Thomson, Spaulding, and Kerr, and to all my old friends. And believe me to remain,

Very sincerely yours,
HENRY C. CRONIN.

The Rev. George S. Chambers, Pastor of the Pine Street Presbyterian Church, Harrisburg, Pa., sends this cordial greeting :

HARRISBURG, October 23, 1885.

DEAR BRO. KERR: I have just received the bill of fare. It will take them another hundred years to get over it. For think of it! Thomson, and Kerr, and Ormiston, and Crosby, and Hall, and Robinson, and Booth, and Stuart, and Taylor, and Wilson, and Alexander, and Shiland, and Carter, and Hamilton, and Spaulding, and Field, and Chambers, and Rossiter, and Van Dyke, and Prime, and a collation ! It takes one's breath away to look at it. You have evidently great faith in the appropriating and enduring power of the "old Fourth." How I wish I could be there ! But with this go my heartiest and highest wishes for the success of the centennial, and your own prosperity and happiness. Give my warmest regards to Dr. Thomson. I often think of him as the first minister in New-York with whom I got acquainted; who introduced me to the New-York Presbytery ; who was such a kind and wise counselor; who was so ready to help a young minister when in a tight place; and who always welcomed me to his home. I often have thought of our fellowship, and have wished that I could meet him again.

May you have a grand, good time,—and you certainly will if there is anything in the hopes and prayers of Yours fraternally,

GEORGE S. CHAMBERS.

Another letter is from the Rev. Archibald McCullagh, D. D., Pastor of the Ross Street Presbyterian Church, Brooklyn, N. Y.

135 BEDFORD AVENUE, BROOKLYN,
October 26, 1885.

MY DEAR BRO. KERR: Accept my hearty congratulations that your church has completed her hundredth year, and under your efficient ministry is still young, strong, vigorous, and progressive as at any previous period of her existence. I hope the centennial exercises may not only prove interesting in themselves, but be productive of lasting good, and tend to widen the sphere of the influence of your church in the years which are to come.

Yours sincerely,
ARCHIBALD McCULLAGH.

The Rev. John B. Dales, D. D., Secretary of the Board of Foreign Missions of the United Presbyterian Church in North America, writes:

136 North 18th Street, Philadelphia,
October 28, 1885.

Dear Dr. Kerr: Yesterday I was called to visit your city to attend a meeting of the American portion of the Commission of the Presbyterian Alliance. While there I heard at length of the good time you and your people are having this week; and, being in the large list of your friends here and elsewhere, I would, if my hurried time had at all allowed, have gone to your house and been at some one, at least, of your meetings. You are, my dear brother, to be congratulated, as I most earnestly do congratulate you, upon being permitted to sing so much of goodness and mercy in your pastoral charge. Your people have had an honored and useful history, and they do truly nobly and well in commemorating as they do this week the covenant faithfulness and goodness of the God of their fathers and their own God. Most earnestly do I join my prayer with many others that the past may be but as the beginning and the precursor of many, very many, years of still more and more enriching blessing.

In his sovereign providence, God took you to that charge, and I have rejoiced in hearing from time to time of your having cheering and comforting tokens of His favor. May that happiest of all joys for a pastor be ever largely yours, viz., the joy of seeing souls saved, your people love you, and the children of God edified and fitted for glory through your instrumentality there.

Ever yours very truly,

J. B. Dales.

From France come the congratulatory words of the Rev. W. W. Newell, Jr., the devoted worker in the MacAll Mission at Paris.

Mission Populaire Evangélique de France.

R. W. McALL, 32, Rue Pierre-Guérin,
  Auteuil-Paris, October 16, 1885.

VERY DEAR DR. KERR: Permit me to send to you and to your dear people a word of greeting. You told me that on the last days of October you expected to celebrate the one hundredth birthday of your church. So old and yet so young; as young, as vigorous, as lovely as in the days of your youth; pastor and people younger to-day than ten years ago; literally renewing your youth.

Go on, dear friends, in this mysterious life of grace, adding century to century, yet adding ever force and beauty, a century-plant sending forth constant blossoms, bearing daily fruit. Abraham and Sarah laughed that they should have a son when they were a hundred years old. May you, like them, be blessed with the seed the Lord hath promised you. And may those born of God among you occupy the world for Christ.

Many lands bless you to-day; many souls pray for you. And France, who has felt the quickening impulse of your sympathy and prayer and endeavor, begs to speak to you her thanks; and little among the multitude of your friends, even I may love you and pray for you and thank God for you.

Very sincerely yours in the ever-living Church,
  WILLIAM NEWELL, JR.

The Rev. JOSEPH KERR, D. D., and Church.

EXTRACTS OF PRESS NOTICES.

The New-York *Observer* said:

FOURTH PRESBYTERIAN CHURCH CENTENNIAL.

The Fourth Presbyterian Church of this city, now under the pastoral care of Rev. Joseph R. Kerr, is celebrating its centennial during the present week. On Sunday morning the Rev. John Thomson, D. D., of Scotland, who was pastor from 1851 to 1864, with an interval of four years, preached. In the afternoon the Rev. Dr. Kerr preached an historical discourse of great interest, giving the annals of the church from its foundation in 1785 to the present time, and also a detailed report of the work which has been accomplished by this organization since its commencement.

This discourse is to be published in full, and will be a valuable addition to the historical records of the churches of the city.

The centennial services continue every evening of the present week, ministers and laymen of various denominations taking part.

(From the New-York *Evangelist.*)

The Fourth Presbyterian Church is commemorating the completion of its first century, it having been organized in the autumn of 1785, just at the close of the Revolution. The pastor, Dr. Joseph R. Kerr, has had printed a handsome, broad-paged invitation, and also programme of the proceedings, which will be preserved by very many as one of the souvenirs of the occasion. The centennial services began on Sunday, Oct. 25th, and continued through the week, concluding on the following Lord's day, Nov. 1st, with the Sacrament of the Lord's Supper, at 4 P. M., conducted by Rev. Drs. Thomson, Spaulding, and the pastor.

The *Scottish-American Journal*, the organ of the Scottish residents of this country, gave a lengthy historical account of the church and the centenary, from which is taken the following:

One Hundred Years Old.

The centennial exercises of the Fourth Presbyterian Church, this city, commenced on Sabbath morning last in presence of a congregation which completely filled the large building on West Thirty-fourth Street. Old friends of the church from far and near were there in large numbers, and the reunion was most impressive. They were warmly welcomed by the present members of the congregation. The sacred edifice was very tastefully decorated with a large assortment of plants, leaves, etc., and their beautiful autumnal tints had a very pleasing effect. Over the pulpit were placed prominently the dates 1785 and 1885. The Rev. Dr. John Thomson, formerly pastor of the church, occupied the pulpit, and preached a practical and earnest discourse from the text in John xvii. 22 —"The glory which thou gavest me, I have given to them." His theme was the priceless privilege of being blessed of the Lord with saving grace.

The church was again crowded at the afternoon service.

The sermon took the form of an historical discourse by the Rev. Dr. Joseph R. Kerr, the pastor of the church, whose text was from Deuteronomy xxxii. 7 — "Remember the days of old; consider the years of generation and generation." Dr. Kerr traced the history of the church from its humble beginning until the present time, when it holds an honored position among the active working churches within the bounds of the Presbytery of New-York. The exercises were of a very interesting character, and congratulatory to the Christian work done by the Fourth Presbyterian Church in New-York during the last hundred years.

In all, it is a most delightful season in the history of the Fourth Church.

The meetings were favorably noticed from day to day by the *Times*, the *Herald*, the *World*, the *Mail and Express*, and the *Evening Telegram*, and thus public interest was sustained up to the closing service.

THESE Centennial Services were largely attended, business and social engagements gave way, while old and young heartily united in making the occasion a splendid success.

The music was conducted by Mr. W. A. Place and Mr. J. H. Munro, assisted by a trained volunteer choir.

The ushers were under the direction of Mr. W. H. Harrison, and the programme-distributers were lads from our Sabbath schools.

The church was elaborately decorated with autumnal foliage, palms, and flowering plants. In front of the desk was a large floral Bible, and on the walls were the suggestive figures, 1785–1885.

Thus a memorable period in our history has been commemorated, and it is hoped that as often as these pages are perused, something of the pleasure and profit of this happy week may be enjoyed by the reader.

The engravings of the churches at Grand and Mercer streets and Grand and Crosby streets were executed and presented by one of our young lady members, Miss Emma S. Haslett.

The preparation of this Record of the Centennial Anniversary was referred, with power, to the Pastor and the Printing Committee.

www.ingramcontent.com/pod-product-compliance
Lightning Source LLC
Chambersburg PA
CBHW031814220426
43662CB00007B/646